NEW YORK METROPOLITAN REGION STUDY

RAYMOND VERNON, DIRECTOR

A STUDY UNDERTAKEN BY THE GRADUATE
SCHOOL OF PUBLIC ADMINISTRATION,
HARVARD UNIVERSITY, FOR
REGIONAL PLAN ASSOCIATION, INC.

Max Hall, Editorial Director

THE
NEWCOMERS

NEGROES AND PUERTO RICANS
IN A CHANGING METROPOLIS

By Oscar Handlin

HARVARD UNIVERSITY PRESS
Cambridge, Massachusetts · 1959

Endpaper map by Jeanyee Wong

Designed by Marcia R. Lambrecht

Library of Congress Catalog Card Number 59–14737

Printed in the United States of America

For the Memory of
ELLIOT E. COHEN
who was ever eager
to understand American society

Foreword

This is one of a series of books on the forces that shape metropolitan areas. In particular, the series has to do with the forces that shape the largest and most complex metropolitan area in the United States, a 22-county expanse which takes in parts of three states but which, for convenience, we have termed the New York Metropolitan Region.

In 1956, the Regional Plan Association, Inc., a nonprofit research and planning agency whose purpose is to promote the coordinated development of these 22 counties, requested the Graduate School of Public Administration of Harvard University to undertake a three-year study of the Region. The challenging task was to analyze the key economic and demographic features of the Region and to project them to 1965, 1975, and 1985.

The resulting studies are reports to the Regional Plan Association. At the same time, they are designed to be of service to a much broader audience. Most Americans now live in metropolitan areas; indeed, ever-increasing proportions of the world's populations are gravitating to metropolitan clusters. Their well-being depends to a considerable extent on how these areas develop. Yet the scholar's understanding of the currents underlying the rise of such areas seems grossly inadequate.

As a study of these underlying currents, this project is neither a blueprint for action nor an analysis of metropolitan government. It has no recommendations to make about the physical structure of the Region or about the form or activities of the governmental bodies there. At the same time, it is a necessary prelude to future planning studies of the Region and to well considered recommendations for governmental action. Its end product is an analysis of the Region's probable development, assuming that the economic and demographic forces in sight follow their indicated course and assuming that the role of government is largely limited to existing policies.

The results of the Study, it is hoped, will be applied in many ways. Governments and enterprises in the Region should be in a better position to plan their future programs if they become more closely aware of the economic environment in which they may expect to operate. Other metropolitan areas, it is already evident, will benefit from the methodology and the conclusions which the Study has developed.

From the first, there has been a general recognition that the main part of the Study would have to be done by a group located within the New York Metropolitan Region and devoted exclusively to the project. Such a group was assembled in New York. The work that followed was a complex partnership. The New York staff functioned in close harness with members of the Harvard University faculty. It drew on the faculties of other universities, including Columbia University, Fordham University, Hofstra College, New York University, and Rutgers University. It obtained the help of dozens of governmental organizations in the Region and literally hundreds of private groups and individuals. It made use of the materials which the Regional Plan Association had painstakingly pulled together in prior years.

Each book in the series has a place in the total structure of the Study; yet each is designed to be a complete work in itself. The final report, containing the synthesis and projections of the Study, is scheduled for publication sometime in 1960.

It is not easy to account for all the elements that went into the making of this book nor of the others in the series. The Regional Plan Association performed an indispensable function in conceiving and sponsoring the idea of a study. The Ford Foundation and the Rockefeller Brothers Fund generously provided the financial support. The usual formula in such a situation obviously applies: credit for the Study's results must be shared with those who helped to bring it about, but the onus of error or omission lies with us.

The several volumes in the series bear the names of their principal authors. The undertaking as a whole has been under the direction of Raymond Vernon. He is responsible for the final report and substantial parts of other studies, and his guidance is evident throughout the series.

EDWARD S. MASON
for the Graduate School
of Public Administration,
Harvard University.

Contents

TABLES

CONTENTS

CHART

The Newcomers

I

Introduction

It is often necessary in social science to obscure reality in the interest of clarity of analysis. The generalizations that make prediction possible cannot simply be elicited from the complex of interrelationships which constitute the world of actuality. It is not possible, for instance, to understand the forces that operate within a modern community by regarding it in its totality. Those forces will yield to analysis only if they are isolated as discrete variables and treated apart from the social context within which they are in actuality imbedded.

This procedure, essential as it is, nevertheless also presents the danger that it may be confused with reality. The models which emerge from the process of analysis and generalization are not identical with any actual situation; to serve usefully as instruments of prediction they must be measured against the complex elements of the situation excluded in the process of the analysis.

To study a community like New York it is necessary to deal with its components as if they were integers altogether comparable one with another. One can measure growth, for example, only through such abstractions as "population," a term which implies that the units within it are sufficiently alike to be counted. Yet it would be deceptive in speaking of the population of a city to forget that it is actually compounded of numerous dissimilar groups which are themselves but congeries of unique individuals. It is essential in dealing with the city's population to keep distinctly in mind the respects in which its elements are and are not comparable.

Among the factors that differentiate the residents of the twentieth-century American metropolis are the cultural and social dissimilarities derived from the heterogeneity of their ethnic origins. Since urban growth has been largely the product of immigration from outside the city limits, a diverse and mixed population has always been characteristic of these places. Differences in origin have influenced many aspects of urban life; and it will be difficult to explain the development of the past or to project that of the future without taking account of those differences.

It is particularly necessary to do so in the case of New York, one of the most cosmopolitan of American cities. In any consideration of the future of the metropolitan region * of which New York is the center, the question inevitably arises of what effect the distinctive composition of its population will have.

At the moment, that question is most immediately raised by the growing number of Negroes and Puerto Ricans in the area. The problems of adjustment of these recent newcomers to the city have produced a sense of shock among many of their neighbors who regard their difficulties as altogether unprecedented in the development of the metropolis. The shock, curiously, is as great among New Yorkers who are themselves children or grandchildren of immigrants as among the descendants of the oldest stocks.[1]

The dismay with which these groups are viewed is in part due to the fact that they involve the city in the question of color; and that has serious connotations to all Americans in the 1950's. But, more important in explaining the shock at the presence of the Negroes and Puerto Ricans is the inability to view these people in the perspective of the city's earlier experience. The inference of a good deal of contemporary discussion is that these problems are altogether new and therefore insoluble.

Yet the problems of the marginal wage earner, of substandard housing, or of juvenile delinquency are by no means novel in the

* The region, as defined for this study, consists of twenty-two counties ranging from Fairfield County, Connecticut, on the northeast to Monmouth County, New Jersey, on the southwest; this area includes the seventeen counties of the Standard Metropolitan Area as defined by the Bureau of the Census and, in addition, five outlying counties.

history of New York. There are enough precedents for them in the early experience of the city and the more recent development of the region so that an understanding of the past may offer a useful guide to the expectations of the future. To that end it is necessary to recall rather than to push away the recollection of that past.

The method of this effort to comprehend the situation of present-day New York ethnic groups will therefore be largely historical. An examination of the population of the city in terms of its ethnic characteristics may isolate and define the problems involved in the adjustment of immigrants to urban life; it may also supply a basis for assessing the earlier consequences for the community of the presence of groups comparable to those which now trouble it.

Such an examination will provide a useful background for an analysis of the major streams of migration in the past thirty years. The question will then be raised as to whether and how the Negroes and Puerto Ricans of the first three decades are significantly different from the immigrants of the first three hundred years of New York's history. That comparison will make it possible to project a line of future development that may be helpful in understanding the character of the community as a whole.

2

The Historical Background, 1620–1928

A COLONIAL MARKETPLACE, 1620–1820

In its first century and a half, New York was a colonial town, dependent upon imperial connections, both for the trade by which it lived and for many necessities of social and cultural life. Yet the peculiar character of its situation encouraged the development within the city of the diversified population that was to be characteristic of it in the future.

The Dutch West India Company established the fortified trading post of New Amsterdam on the tip of Manhattan Island in order to profit from the advantageous relation of the site to the West Indies. From this base, the Hollanders expected to be able to do business with, or raid, the wealthy Spanish colonies. Through their tenure, commercial strategy dominated the policy of the Company with regard to the population.

Holland itself, of course, had a reputation for tolerance in the early seventeenth century; and the desire to develop trade made for laxity overseas also. The Dutch were not so much concerned with building up a settled community like that of their homeland. They were more interested in strengthening the business enterprise of the province. Therefore, they tolerated or even encouraged the arrival of merchants of every type. They negligently allowed New Englanders to encroach upon Long Island and Westchester and permitted a group of Jews fleeing from Brazil to make their homes in New Amsterdam. In addition, they brought in Negro servants to labor for them. These three groups were rather substantial in size by 1660 and they were supplemented by scattered handfuls of other strangers.[1]

Changes in the control of the colony, therefore, had relatively little effect on the population. The English seized New Amsterdam in 1664, then in the next few years lost and reconquered it. These fluctuations in government did not greatly agitate the residents of the town who went about their business without excessive concern about who were their masters.

One hundred years of English rule did not fundamentally alter the situation. In that period New York grew to be a great seaport. Its position was still remarkably favorable. It was close to the trade of the West Indies and able to deal directly with England and Europe. And in the Hudson River Valley it had a fertile back country that supplied it with grains and furs that were valuable staples of trade in the eighteenth century.

Within this commercial community, every type of man was at home. The total population grew rapidly, especially after 1730; and within it there was room for a variety of nationalities that perpetuated the heterogeneity of the city. The Dutch and English, descendants of the former and present rulers of the colony were most numerous. But there were also Huguenot, Jewish, and German communities; and the number of Negro slaves grew with some rapidity.[2]

Nor did the Revolution fundamentally alter the pattern of this development. Between 1776 and 1815 there were disturbances of considerable importance in trade. The War of Independence and the series of Anglo-French conflicts after 1793 broke up the older international commercial system. But New York did better than any other American city during this period of distress. During the Revolution it was long held by the British and thus able to do business with England when its rivals could not. And, later, its favorable situation continued to give it an advantage in trade.[3]

As a result its population grew steadily on into the nineteenth century. Only the number of Negro slaves showed a perceptible decline after 1780, as the fleeing loyalists took their bondsmen with them.

But the growth in the number of free people of color more than made up for that. The long succession of Anglo-French wars kept the volume of foreign immigration relatively low until after 1815. But the existing variety of different ethnic groups remained characteristic of the city.[4]

With the restoration of peace after Waterloo, New York profited still more by the development of trans-Atlantic trade. The British merchants chose it as the market into which to dump their accumulated wares after 1815. New York thereafter became the chief gateway for commerce between the United States and England; and the city quickly resumed its rapid growth. In 1820, its population had mounted to more than 123,000. After 1815, also, the tide of immigration, long suspended by the European wars, began to flow again. A substantial percentage of those who arrived in America entered by way of New York; and many of them stayed there.[5]

For the first two hundred years of its development, therefore, New York had been a cosmopolitan city. A thriving seaport that lived by its contact with the outside world, it was accustomed to making room for the elements of foreign birth who had long been present and familiar there.

The city's diverse groups encountered relatively little difficulty of adjustment. Among the newcomers were a substantial number of merchants who fitted readily into the commercial community which they strengthened by their activities. The German John Jacob Astor and the Scotsmen Archibald Gracie and Robert Lenox easily took places at the sides of their English and Huguenot competitors. Most of the other immigrants were also welcomed for their skills and man power.

Only the small group of unskilled laborers, and among them particularly the Negroes, encountered any difficulty. The free colored people had grown steadily more numerous after independence; but they remained an unskilled and turbulent group and something of a problem. Toward the very end of the period, after 1815, when the number of unskilled foreign-born laborers increased, they too began to meet difficulty in settlement.[6]

In a trading town, the opportunities for the employment of un-skilled labor were relatively small and inelastic; and as the supply increased, whether it was white or black, it seemed to create prob-lems of pauperism and delinquency. The rising expense of main-taining the poor strangers troubled the municipal authorities and philanthropic citizens and led to complaints about the character of the new immigrants. In 1819, when there were only 5,000 foreigners in the city, the managers of the Society for the Prevention of Pauper-ism, bewailed the fact that:

This inlet of pauperism threatens us with the most overwhelming con-sequences. From various causes, the city of New York is doomed to be the landing place of a great portion of the European population, who are daily flocking to our country for a place of permanent abode. This city is the greatest importing capital of the United States, and a position from which a departure into the interior is generally considered the most easy and practicable. On being possessed of a more extensive and active trade than any other commercial emporium in the union, it naturally occurs to the minds of emigrants that we possess more means of employment. Our situation is peculiarly healthy, and no local objection either physical or moral, exists, to arrest the approach of foreigners. The present state of Europe contributes in a thousand ways to vast and unceasing emigration to the United States. A universal shock of commercial embarrassment has pervaded, and still pervades the continent of Europe. The whole system of trade and exchange is affected; internal industry directed to new objects; nations are manufacturing for themselves, and abandoning the usual resorts; armies and navies are disbanded, and labor-saving machin-ery is daily lessening the necessity of manual industry. Hence an almost innumerable population beyond the ocean is cast out of employment, and this has the effect of increasing the usual want of employ. This county is the resort of vast numbers of these needy and wretched beings. . . . Many of them arrive here destitute of every thing. . . . Instead of seek-ing the interior, they cluster in our cities, or sojourn along our seaboard, depending on the incidents of time, charity, or depredation, for subsist-ence. . . . More than twenty-eight thousand . . . have arrived at this port in twenty months. . . . Many of these foreigners may have found employment; some may have passed into the interior; but thousands still remain among us. They are frequently found destitute in our streets; they seek employment at our doors; they are found in our almshouse, and in our hospitals; they are found at the bar of our criminal tribunals, in our bridewell, our penitentiary, and our state prison. And we lament to say, that they are too often led by want, by vice, and by habit, to form a phalanx of plunder and depredation, rendering our city more liable to the increase of crimes, and our houses of correction, more crowded with convicts and felons.

The managers warned that immigration would continue for generations and would threaten the city with a moral contagion. Like many troubled New Yorkers in the next one hundred and forty years they could not understand how the newcomers could "be suddenly identified with ourselves and our children." [7]

Nevertheless, even such complaints were not directed against immigration as such, only against its apparent abuses. There was no suggestion that further admissions be restricted; nor any general feeling of hostility to the newcomers. The remedy for the disorder seemed to be more adequate financial guarantees to relieve the burden on the city's taxpayers. The certainty of future growth was so firmly held and the conception of the diversity of the population was so thoroughly ingrained in the city that there was no serious challenge to the principle of complete freedom of entry.

In retrospect these fears seem an exaggerated reflection of the city's growing pains. At the end of the eighteenth century it had been still a tight little settlement clustered at the tip of Manhattan Island. A line along Stanton Street, Broadway, and Leonard Street would have taken in almost the whole built-up district. In 1808 when the City Hall was erected it was on the outskirts of town. A decade later, it had been engulfed by the spread of population. [8]

Neither the supply of housing nor of municipal services could keep up with this rapid growth. In the resultant overcrowding, the poorest elements suffered the most; there was already a resort to the cellar dwellings that would prove disastrous later. In 1820, 562 Negroes lived on Banker (later Madison) Street, 119 of them in cellars. When the fever struck that year, 70 of them died, and 155 others were ill. This was a token of the far greater difficulties of the next half-century. [9]

THE EMPIRE CITY, 1820–1870

The fifty years between 1820 and 1870 witnessed the unparalleled expansion of New York's commerce and with it the rapid increase in the number of the city's residents. The growth of both trade and population involved heavier immigration than ever before, which in turn confirmed the diverse character of the city's society. In this period also many of the characteristics of urban settlement in New York would be firmly established.

New York's prosperity was based on its strategic situation at the intersection of a number of significant routes of trade. The most important was that which ran east and west from the markets of England to the interior of the American continent. Along it moved grains and other American raw materials in exchange for the manufactured goods of Europe. New York had the advantage of easy access to the rich back country of the interior West. By 1830, to the Mohawk Valley settlements had been added those of the Hudson River Valley. Before mid-century all of western New York State and much of Ohio, Indiana, and Illinois were also tributary to the city. The completion of the Erie Canal in 1825 gave the metropolis an unsurpassable competitive advantage in bringing goods out of the interior. Try as they might, none of its rivals—Boston, Philadelphia, or Baltimore—could compete successfully against it.

Another line of trade was coastal. It carried northward the cotton and tobacco of the southern states to be shipped by way of New York either to New or old England and, in exchange, brought to the South manufactured goods from the mills of New England and of old England. The intersection of these routes of trade at New York gave it an incomparably favorable situation. On the eve of the Civil War, it handled 70 per cent of the nation's imports and 33 per cent of the exports.

Changes in transportation in the 1840's and 1850's confirmed the city's strategic position. The line of railroads up the Hudson River and westward to the Great Lakes, while not altogether integrated or controlled by New York, nevertheless served the interests of the port and aided business enterprise. Finally, the appearance of manufacturing outside the traditional handicraft forms added to the city's prosperity. Already in the 1820's, shipbuilding and sugar refining were large-scale industries. After 1830, the fabrication of ready-made clothing became increasingly important and, in the 1850's, was producing a product valued at some $20,000,000.[10]

This economic development was dependent upon a rapid expansion of population.[11] As earlier, continued immigration from a variety of sources contributed to the city's growth. Of the extremely important contingent from within the United States, the most significant elements were those which migrated from New England and which long constituted a remarkably cohesive group within the population of New York. The Grinnell, Low, Peck, and Phelps families among others assumed significant roles in the commercial life of the city; and many other Yankees held lesser positions as clerks, artisans, and shopkeepers.[12]

There were also minor additions to the Negro population of the city, which rose from a little more than 10,000 in 1820 to 12,569 in 1860. That growth was not due to natural increase but to migration; indeed the number of colored natives of New York City in 1860 was smaller than the number of Negroes in 1820. Yet the metropolis was attractive to newcomers. Emancipation in New York State was complete in 1827 and, although the blacks were still subject to many disabilities, the superior attractions of New York drew substantial numbers from neighboring middle states and from New England. Moreover, the thriving trade with the South opened important channels for the movement to the city of free Negroes and fugitive slaves.[13]

This small and rather stable group had relatively few difficulties in adjustment. The Negroes became barbers, sailors, coachmen, cooks, servants, and caterers; and, while not many became wealthy, they had a secure place in the service trades. They lived in a cluster on Mulberry Street with a scattering uptown; and they had already developed a coherent communal life that centered in the African Methodist and the Abyssinian Baptist churches. They had genuine grievances, such as their segregation in a separate school, but these seemed minor in comparison with the burdens of colored people elsewhere.[14]

But the most important groups of immigrants were those who now came from Europe.[15] In the first twenty years after 1820, these were predominantly of a type very similar to those of the eighteenth century. The Englishmen, Frenchmen, and Germans who arrived in those two decades were mostly farmers and artisans who sought more attractive opportunities in the New World and who had the resources necessary to bring them across. Many remained in the city but briefly before moving out to the West. Those who stayed were primarily skilled and entered into the artisan life of the community.

Quite another element became increasingly important after 1840. The new movement was set in motion by the difficulties of life in Ireland and Germany. In both countries, agriculture was shifting rapidly away from its traditional communal forms toward large-scale capitalist organization. In the process, substantial groups of landless peasants were displaced and lost their stake in society. At first they drifted about as hired laborers; but soon many of them began to find room in the ships that came to the New World. The great potato famines of 1846–1848 in both Ireland and Germany increased their numbers remarkably and also gave an urgency to their desire to escape.[16]

These people had no choice of destination. They were almost unique in the history of immigration in their intense desire to flee to America; whatever conditions they would discover in the New World were preferable to the starvation of the Old. They simply followed the shipping lines and came wherever their vessels went. Furthermore, few of them had the resources to move beyond the seaports. They were totally immobilized at the docks where they debarked. As a result, despite ambitious schemes to spread them into the interior, a large percentage (20–30 per cent) remained in New York City.[17] The immigrant population of the town consequently rose rapidly. By 1870 there were more than 400,000 foreign-born in the city, well over 44 per cent of its inhabitants. Most numerous were the Irish and Germans, who, in 1855, formed 28 per cent and 15 per cent of the total residents respectively. But the city also held groups of lesser importance from every other nation of Europe.[18]

The character of the new immigration markedly influenced the economic adjustment of the newcomers. The minority of craftsmen and merchants among them who brought skills or capital with them to the New World were able, as in the earlier period, to establish themselves after an initial period of apprenticeship. Such people still found the labor market favorable to them. But the displaced landless peasants who formed a large percentage of both the Irish and German immigrants lacked either resources or skill. The handicrafts were consequently closed to them; and, since they had only their labor to sell, the city offered them few opportunities. They became porters, sweepers, and construction workers; and their wives and children went into service or began to take in sewing or laundry. But the result of their toiling did not raise them above the most marginal existence.[19]

Only a few of these laborers had the capacity ultimately to rise to more secure or more remunerative situations on the police force or in other menial branches of government service. The mass of them were more likely, if they found steady employment at all, to do so in the new large-scale industries, like clothing manufacture. By 1855, of some 20,000 employees in those industries, fully 9,128 were Irish and 8,307 were Germans. But, since these branches of manufacturing thrived by the cheapness of their labor supply, earnings were minimal; and the laborers who depended upon them for their existence remained perennially poverty-stricken.[20]

The appearance of a large, resourceless, and poor laboring population markedly influenced the whole city. As the population grew, settlement spread rapidly northward, moving approximately one mile a decade along the diagonal of Broadway, somewhat more rapidly on the West than on the East Side. By 1840, the built-up area had reached 14th Street; by 1850, 34th Street; and, by 1860, 42nd Street.[21]

Three dynamic factors conditioned the spread of settlement and permanently influenced the patterns of land use in the city. The newest arrivals, who accepted the cheapest accommodations, tended to replace the more prosperous earlier residents who moved away from the original centers toward the suburbs of the city. In the development of the neighborhoods, ethnic groups tended to cluster together. In the process of redistribution of the population, occasional islands of a fixed character resisted the invasions of outsiders and compelled the moving line of settlement to leap erratically over them.

The growth of population and the rapid obsolescence of old buildings had always created a persistent shortage of housing in the city. That shortage had been compounded by disastrous fires in 1835 and 1845. Thereafter, facilities were totally incapable of keeping up with the growth of population. The latest immigrants were the poorest element in the city and had the least mobility. They had no choice but to accept whatever residences were cheapest. Furthermore, as strangers they were reluctant to venture far from the place at which they landed; and, as casual laborers insecure in employment, they felt a compulsion to remain near the mercantile districts where the jobs were.

These people therefore tended at first to accumulate in the districts of the First and Second Wards that backed up against the East River docks. There, in the midst of the most active business district of the city, they could find temporary quarters in numerous boarding houses.

There, too, housing of a more permanent character was becoming available. Many old homes were vacated by their former occupants as the whole area became unattractive as a place of residence. The poor already there made unpleasant neighbors; and the encroachment of business enterprises, with their bustling warehouses, steadily blighted the edges of the region. This area was surrounded by a crowded commercial district and bordered by the Kolk or Collect Pond, which had been a swamp even in the eighteenth century and had now become a noisome reservoir of the city's sewage and rub-

bish; any one who had the choice fled from it. By 1840, the central
district of immigrant settlement had spread north to take in the
Sixth Ward and the Five Points district.[22]

Here a pattern of cheap lodging developed to accommodate the
immigrants. Land was high in speculative value; owners were less
inclined to make repairs than to allow old buildings to deteriorate
until they could be sold and torn down, especially if they could in
the meantime earn a good income in rent. Sublandlords or con-
tractors took over the old commercial and residential structures and
converted them into multiple-family dwellings. They used space that
had formerly been left uneconomically vacant, built barracks in the
back yards, and turned the cellars into apartments. By a marvel of
ingenuity, for instance, an old brewery in the Five Points became
home to more than two hundred souls. Accepting transients, renting
at weekly terms, making no repairs, the entrepreneurs were able to
derive a much higher income than from more respectable use of the
property. The immigrants received accommodations of a sort at a
price in money within their reach; the cost in health, they could not
reckon.[23]

As the population grew, the formerly pleasant residential streets
were transformed into slums and the old occupants fled to the outskirts of town. The process was cumulative; the flight of some made
more housing available to newcomers, which led to further deterioration and to the flight of more. Young people and those who could
not immediately afford residences in good areas took up boarding
house and hotel life until they could properly establish themselves
and escape to the outlying regions of town.

The barrier of the Collect Pond and the ease of movement along
Broadway induced the old residents to move to the Northwest, first
to Greenwich Village, where a nucleus had already developed after
the yellow fever epidemics of 1819–1823. This became known as the
American Ward in the 1840's. Then, as settlement progressed, other
natives found residences even farther away, in the more northerly
regions of the island. In the 1830's some had already built country
homes in Bloomingdale, a pleasant village on the Hudson at 100th

Street, or further north at Manhattanville (125th Street). Others began to use the ferries to get to Brooklyn Heights or to New Jersey.
The pressure increased in the 1850's as the area of densest settlement
spread outward. A parallel movement passed up the east side to
Murray Hill and Harlem, which commuters could reach by a lei-
surely one-hour ride on the horsecars. By then, moreover, Brooklyn,
which became a city in 1834, was also crowded, as its population
mounted above 100,000; and those who sought rustic quiet were
compelled to build their villas in Staten Island and Flatbush.[24]

The whole movement was ethnic in character. That does not mean
that the population simply sorted itself out territorially by homogeneous groups. People of every nationality were scattered throughout the city. No ward was purely homogeneous. Nor was any group
confined to a single quarter of town. But those who moved tended
to seek out and to settle with people like themselves. Neighborhoods
thus acquired a character defined by their churches, shops, and facilities for leisure and entertainment; and individuals with a common
background were attracted by common facilities. When the older residents moved, the New England Yankees tended to cluster in one
section, the Quakers in another, and the Jews in a third.[25]

As some Irish and Germans also acquired the means to move out
of the central district, they followed the same pattern. Both spread
to the east, the Irish below East Broadway, the Germans above it.
There they established a Little Ireland and a Little Germany.

But the ability of those communities to expand was limited by the
entrenchment around them of other groups. The Irish spread to the
north as far as Houston Street, but beyond that were halted by
the solid barrier of Greenwich Village. They were compelled to skip
that neighborhood and to move north of Fourteenth Street up the
West Side into the region that came to be known as Hell's Kitchen.
Others went eastward by ferry to Brooklyn. Similarly the Germans
were forced to remain on the east side of the Island. When space
became tight there they also moved across the river to Brooklyn,
Williamsburgh, and Greenpoint, places linked by ferries to their old
areas of residence.

In addition, on the outskirts of town were shanty settlements where squatters without legal titles made their homes. By 1860, the German "Dutch Hill" on the East River between 38th and 44th Streets matched the Irish shanty towns a little further north on the Hudson.[26]

The migration created vast problems of urban living. Standards of sanitation under these conditions collapsed. Not until 1842 was Croton water introduced in the city and it was a long time thereafter before it extended into the tenement districts. At the end of the period it had still not been brought into most of the homes of the poor. In the 1850's two-thirds of the city was still unprovided with sewers. Cellar dwellings which then housed 29,000 people were subject to frequent flooding and became pestilential from the want of drainage. It was not surprising therefore to find a marked rise in disease even in normal times; and that altogether apart from the frequent occasions when disastrous epidemics struck as the cholera did in 1832, 1843, 1849, and 1855. Even in normal years there was a rapid increase in consumption, typhus, typhoid fever, and cholera, so that the mortality rate rose to a murderous peak of 1 : 27.15 in 1857. The foreign-born always contributed a disproportionate share to the mortality rolls.[27]

Other disorders were also troublesome. There was undoubtedly a rise in the incidence of crime and of juvenile delinquency, although statistics are unreliable and it is difficult to assess the degree to which the deterioration was the product of immigration. Already in 1824 there were complaints that the "increasing numbers and deplorable situation" of the city's juvenile offenders "call for the more effective interposition of its police." Yet, the very persistence of those complaints through the next century and a third indicated that the problem was more a characteristic of urban growth than of the character of the people who were immigrating.[28]

Some forms of delinquency seem altogether independent of the particular ethnic groups who were, from time to time, caught up in them. Organized gambling, for instance, became a major problem before 1850; the policy games that survived until the present had by then taken form. But, while immigrants participated in the games of chance, they were not excessively prominent either as victims or as promoters.[29]

On the other hand, some groups showed a particular susceptibility to one social disorder or another. The Irish were disproportionately involved in pauperism and crime. In the 1840's it was almost automatically assumed that an orphan was Irish. Forming 28 per cent of the population of the city in the 1850's, these people accounted for fully 69 per cent of the pauperism and 55 per cent of the arrests. The Germans, by contrast, who were 10 per cent of the population, contributed 10 per cent of both arrests and paupers.[30] In part, the discrepancy can be explained by the greater poverty of the Irish. But the Germans were also poorly prepared for urban life and suffered also from the effects of low incomes and inadequate housing. Additional cultural sources of social weakness must have contributed to the disruption of family life and the loss of control responsible for these forms of delinquency.[31]

The men and women involved in the trying problems of rapid community change were, however, rarely in a position to reason abstractly about causes. The situation created a high degree of tension marked by intervals of open hostility toward the immigrants from the 1830's onward. Some of that ill-feeling sprang from the resentment of native artisans against their foreign-born competitors.[32] More generally, it embodied anxieties about an unknown future of which the strangers were symbols; it then found expression in political movements directed against the immigrants and more specifically against the Irish Catholics, who were most alien of all.

But these conflicts did not always array natives against immigrants. Occasionally Germans and Irish and Negroes took sides against one another, as in the events that led to the great riots of July 1863.[33] These outbursts expressed a smoldering discontent with the painful effects of social change.

Yet, significantly, no one questioned the desirability of immigration as such. The nativist organizations sought to limit the political rights of the foreign-born, but not to end the flow of newcomers, closely connected as that was with the growth of the city.[34]

Under the pressure of their difficult situations, people of common background drew together for the satisfaction of common social and cultural needs. Since the city had become so heterogeneous, it no longer was able to satisfy those needs in comprehensive organizations. Mutual aid societies, churches, newspapers, theaters, militia and fire companies, and fraternal societies reflected the diversity of the city's population. By 1840 there were already identifiable English, Scottish, Irish, German, French, Welsh, Spanish, Jewish, and New England organizations. In the next three decades there would be added Scandinavian, Dutch, Belgian, French-Canadian, and Italian ones. Each of these groups was thus in process of establishing an internal communal structure of its own.[35]

There were substantial parallels in structure among all of these voluntary organizations. In each the leadership was primarily in the hands of men who acquired status and authority by their wealth. Businessmen were generally the organizing and dominating elements, although they often operated through functionaries who were clergymen. There were some variations from group to group. Among the Germans, for instance, a relatively small number of intellectuals played a significant role in communal life, particularly after 1848. These men came to America for reasons different from those which influenced the mass of immigrants. But they edited the German newspapers and were active in the group's internal politics and thus exercised a pervasive influence. On the other hand, among the Irish, the paucity of businessmen gave a disproportionate importance to the clergy and to a few individuals who advanced to prominence through politics.[36]

Despite such differences of detail, the common character of their leadership and the common general organization of all groups reflected widespread acceptance of the common middle-class ideals dominant in the society about them. Even the mass of former peasants, who could not in their own lives apply the American axioms of thrift, hard work, advancement, and progress, recognized that these were the keys to respect and status in the United States. That was why their associations quickly took on banking, building and loan, and insurance functions.[37] That was also why union activity was feeble and intermittent.[38] Among the immigrants, the influence of middle-class leadership added force to the general factors that weakened the labor movement in this period. But that same influence was also, generally, a factor that eased intergroup relations and that furthered the adjustment of the newcomers to the situation of the city in which they found themselves.

After the Civil War, there was a slight easing of tension as New York entered upon a new period of rapid expansion. Yet the urban community was still ill prepared to meet the problems of the next decades.

INDUSTRIAL METROPOLIS, 1870–1928

New York continued its growth in the half-century after 1870. Its economic strength supported an ever increasing population and permitted it to spread beyond the boundaries of Manhattan Island, swallowing up in the process a succession of rural communities.[39]

In this period, New York became a great industrial as well as a commercial metropolis. The patterns of trade that had earlier contributed to its strength persisted beyond 1870. Indeed the development of trans-Atlantic commerce after that date tended to magnify New York's advantages and to increase the margin of its superiority over its rivals. The city also consolidated its control over the transcontinental railroad routes and improved its access to the interior of the continent. In addition, New York now became the nation's financial capital; and the activities of its banking and investment houses indirectly stimulated trade. At the end of the century, it enjoyed unchallenged primacy as a seaport.

Apart from these activities which extended earlier lines of development, the city's economy was also sustained by a thriving manufacturing complex. A variety of new industries absorbed an ever-growing labor force. Clothing, printing, and food-processing enterprises grew steadily in size and employed an ever larger number of men and women.[40]

The hands required to operate the rapidly expanding productive system were supplied by a population that mounted with phenomenal rapidity. In the half-century after 1870 it almost quadrupled in size, spilling far beyond the original political boundaries of the city. The central city and the suburbs both grew. The vacant spaces in Manhattan quickly filled up, and nearby Brooklyn and Williamsburgh were crowded by the overflow, particularly after the building of the East River Bridge in 1883.[41]

The annexation of a group of Westchester towns west of the Bronx River in 1874, the addition of some others further east in 1895, and, three years later, the establishment of the consolidated city taking in Brooklyn, Queens, and Richmond reflected the urgent quest for living space. Yet, in 1928, New York had far outrun even these expanded political boundaries and had spread across the nearby areas of Long Island, Westchester County, Connecticut, and New Jersey.

The rise in the number of residents was only to a slight degree due to natural increase. Migration from other parts of the United States (including that by the Negroes which will be discussed later) was more important; but the largest component in the growth of New York's population was derived from European immigration.[42]

There is no way to measure reliably the number of the foreign-born who annually settled in the city. But there are decisive indications that the volume was large, reaching at its maximum almost 200,000 in the single year 1907. The number of newcomers to the United States rose steadily until 1884, then slumped briefly before resuming a new rise that reached its peak in 1907 and persisted on to World War I. In 1919 the movement was resumed only to be cut short by hostile legislation in 1921 and 1924. Of the new arrivals, a substantial percentage expressed the intention of remaining in New York, and, in addition, many more who hoped to go on were persuaded by opportunity or compelled by misfortune to remain. In any case, the number of foreign-born in the city still rose, for the new immigrants more than compensated for the deaths of the old.[43]

As important was the rapid increase in the number of the American-born children of immigrants, who continued to identify themselves with the communities of their parents. In 1890, some 42 per cent of the people in New York City and 32 per cent of those in Brooklyn were foreign born. With their children they constituted a distinct majority of the area's residents. They formed in that year almost 80 per cent of the population of Manhattan Island.

The Irish and German immigration slackened below the level of its earlier peak but persisted at a respectable rate on beyond the turn of the century, the German remaining somewhat higher than the Irish. In 1890, more than 406,000 New Yorkers had at least one Irish, and 426,000 one German, parent.

In addition, after 1870, new sources of immigration mounted in importance. A large and growing Scandinavian contingent was set in motion by economic changes in the homeland. Many of these newcomers made their way to the Middle West, but a substantial number remained in New York City—some of them sailors, and others farmers and peasants attracted by city life.

After 1880, the same social, cultural, and economic transformations spread eastward and southward across the whole face of Europe. Their disturbing impact upon the population of the continent was quickly reflected in a rising volume of emigration to the United States and elsewhere. Although there was some return migration, particularly in the years of depression, the flow did not halt until the war and hostile legislation cut it off.

The Italians and the East European Jews were the most important groups to come to New York. Between 1880 and World War I, a rising population and economic reorganization displaced millions of Italian peasants from their latifundia. Sicily and southern Italy were most heavily affected, and those regions lacked the industrial development which absorbed a similar population in northern Italy. The migrants were peasants without skill or capital and they entered the labor market at its lowest level. By 1890 there were already thousands of them in New York and the number increased steadily thereafter. An estimate of 1903 set the figure at close to 400,000. A high birth rate produced also a large number of second-generation Italians of foreign parents, so that until 1917 the group swelled through both natural increase and emigration. At that date there were probably 730,000 in the city.⁴⁴

The Jews who migrated were set in motion by a combination of religious and economic factors. In Russia, persecution made their position untenable. Discrimination prevented them from leading normal lives, and occasional outbreaks of violence emphasized the precarious nature of their existence. Moreover, their economic situation deteriorated both there and in the Austrian Empire, where persecution was less important. The development of large-scale agriculture and industry destroyed their role as intermediaries between the peasants and the landlords and the urban markets. Thousands became superfluous and fled to America where about half of them settled in New York. Their number increased rapidly after 1890. These East Europeans joined the Jews long since settled in the city but maintained their distinctiveness. Some brought small amounts of capital and skill as traders. But a large majority entered on the lowest rung of the labor ladder.⁴⁵

Smaller, but substantial, groups of new immigrants also appeared from Greece and Rumania, and from the Slavic and Baltic countries. Although they were dwarfed in size by the much larger contingents of Italians and Jews, they represented a very significant element in the total population structure of the city.

The complaints about the stubbornness of the immigrants who persisted in concentrating in New York continued in this period; and there were serious efforts by the government and by private organizations to redistribute them in the interior of the country.⁴⁶ Those complaints were deceptive, for the immigrants after 1880 had more choice of destination than had their predecessors of the 1840's and the 1850's. The whole process of moving was better organized so that the newcomer before leaving home had some idea of where he would go and of what job prospects existed in various parts of the country. Furthermore, the improvement of internal transportation made it possible for immigrants to move to any part of the nation at relatively low cost. And, indeed, they were in fact distributed in other industrial cities as well as in New York. Chicago, Cleveland, St. Louis, and Detroit each received very substantial contributions to its population from the same sources.

The immigrants were drawn to New York not only by the social advantages of nearness to people of their own group, but also—and more important—by the economic opportunities for unskilled labor that existed there. The distribution of the immigrants through the country corresponded almost exactly to the prevalence of such opportunities. The complaints about that distribution really reflected dissatisfaction with the effects of industrialization and focused upon the immigrants as symbols of a change other Americans could not control. The effort to move the immigrants into agriculture ran contrary to the dominant tendencies of the American economy at the end of the nineteenth century. The sons of native farmers were themselves deserting their homesteads to move to the cities; and the immigrants felt the same attraction.[47]

Thus, there was actually a greater relation between immigration and economic opportunity in this period than there had been before 1870. The pool of potential immigrants was built up by forces in Europe that displaced the peasants and pushed them away from their ancestral homes. But the choice of a location and the time of migration were determined largely by the availability of opportunities in the United States. This was most clearly revealed by the growing correspondence between the volume of immigration and the fluctuations of the business cycle. In the earlier period the two had been to some degree independent of each other. Now, the greater availability of information and the greater ease of movement established an ever closer correlation. In addition, the ability to return relieved the American economy of the burden of surplus labor in periods of depression.[48]

The settlement of strangers in New York was never an easy matter. But the newcomers who arrived after 1870 were slightly better off than the immigrants of the 1840's and 1850's. The later arrivals too were unskilled; 80 per cent of them between 1880 and

1890 had no trade. They too lacked capital and found it necessary to adjust to a difficult new economic environment. Like their predecessors they were compelled to struggle for a livelihood by unskilled labor and petty artisanry. But their struggle was eased by the growth of industry. They found positions not only in construction work and in the building trades but also in the expanding manufacturing enterprises. Although there were some tendencies toward concentration—as of Jews and Italian women but not men in the garment industries or of Germans and Bohemians in cigar-making—all labor received a measure of relief by the absorption of some in manufacturing.[49]

For want of alternative, the immigrants took the lowest places in the ranks of industry. They suffered in consequence from the poor pay and miserable working conditions characteristic of the sweatshops and homework in the garment trades and in cigar-making. But they were undoubtedly better off than the Irish and Germans of the 1840's for whom there had been no place at all.[50]

The community paid a considerable social price in the damaging effects of the low wages on which these branches of manufacturing thrived. Yet without the presence of an abundant supply of cheap labor these industries could not have expanded as they did. The 100,000 hands employed in the clothing trades were almost all recent immigrants. Such occupations were open to newcomers because the older residents and their children abandoned them as soon as possible. The sons and daughters of the Irishmen and Germans who had been tailors in the 1850's and 1860's or of the Swedes who had entered that trade in the 1880's did not take up the needle or the iron; and that made employers dependent upon the fresh hands from Italy or Russia.[51]

Escape from the ranks of unskilled labor was, however, not easy and became steadily more difficult. The want of skill and capital was always a handicap. But, in addition, discrimination against the newer ethnic groups grew ever more intense, especially after the turn of the century. These handicaps were particularly burdensome to the second generation. The crucial limitations appeared in the middle ranks of big business as that became more institutionalized.

On the other hand, economic expansion created some channels of upward mobility along which some immigrants and their children could ascend to more desirable places. As earlier, petty trade remained an important avenue of progress. In many neighborhoods the local merchant who sold food his neighbors desired or spoke their language and understood their habits had an advantage even over the emerging chain store. Other immigrants found opportunities in kinds of businesses from which natives withdrew because of the social odium attached to them. Among the Italian, Jewish, and Syrian peddlers of ice, fruit, clothing, dry goods, and junk, who passed along the crowded downtown streets, were some who accumulated the funds to open shops and develop thriving businesses.[52] The independent service trades also offered a start to Italian and Greek barbers and shoemakers and to Jewish tailors.[53] There were, in addition, some means of rising in industry. Wherever contracting was the predominant form of organization, the immigrant—whether an Irish or Jewish boss or an Italian or Greek *padrone*—had an advantage in his access to the labor supply.[54]

A few professional men—doctors, lawyers, pharmacists, clergymen, and politicians—also catered to the needs of the people they understood and who trusted them. The children of the newest arrivals had no more desire to follow their parents' occupations than had earlier generations of Americans.[55] In escaping from the immigrant callings to the professions, they found ties to their ancestral groups, supplemented by education and skills acquired in America, particularly advantageous. The ability to depend upon the support of the group made careers in government and, to a lesser extent, in the church especially attractive to the second generation who in this respect were sometimes better off than the children of the natives.[56]

There were also some small but significant areas of employment in which talent was absolute and surmounted all distinctions of origin. On the stage, in the athletic arena, and in the scientific laboratory, the Irishman or Italian or Jew could demonstrate his worth and establish himself without serious impediment.[57]

Finally, there were opportunities for advancement in businesses of marginal morality, in which immigrants were not restrained by the inhibitions that excluded natives concerned with respectability. Europeans who did not attach to gambling the opprobrium that Americans did quickly took over the policy wheels and other games of chance. Prohibition created the bootlegger; and manpower shortages and hostility to unions, after 1915, made room for the labor racketeer. The logic of the use of violence and of gang organization led the participants in these enterprises into other forms of crime as well and also established an uneasy relation to local politics. But illegality nonetheless provided an attractive means of social advancement, if not always a permanent one.[58]

There were significant differences in the ability of various groups to move out of the ranks of unskilled labor. Although precise measurements are difficult, there is evidence that the mobility of the Jews —given the recency of their arrival—was exceptionally rapid; and that of the Irish—given the length of their residence—was exceptionally slow.[59]

A complex of factors influenced the differences in the rate of social mobility. A comparison of the Irish and the Jewish extremes shows that both groups started low and both were originally limited to such business opportunities as peddling afforded. But the Irish moved upward much more slowly than the Jews. The latter had some experience in trade before emigration, the former did not. The Jews found co-religionists on the spot who were able to help them get established; the earlier Irish immigrants had been peasants no better off than the later. Jewish patterns of family expenditure emphasized the value of saving and eased the process of capital accumulation; Irish surplus earnings were either unprofitably hoarded or expended on higher living standards and on houses which produced no income. With few exceptions, Irish fortunes came from speculative ventures in real estate and from contracting. But beyond these particular factors—important as those were—lay a more general cultural difference which enabled the Jews to orient themselves more purposefully and more quickly to the terms of their new life.[60]

Differential mobility rates became even more important to the second generation. The influence of the initial differences was compounded, as family values shaped the life goals of young people and gave them the means of making a better or worse start. To some degree, family standards influenced attitudes toward education and that in turn was reflected in the extent to which the public school, to which all children were subjected, was stimulating. If the children of Italians in the 1890's and 1920's were inattentive in class, it was not because of want of intelligence but because of lack of incentive; and that proved more of a problem in their studies than unfamiliarity with English. Those who accepted the public school not only acquired valuable skills from it but also values which stressed the importance of the climb upward. For such there were more opportunities to penetrate into the professional and managerial ranks than were open to their contemporaries who either left the school early or were segregated in ethnic parochial schools.[61]

The occupational adjustment of the immigrants was reflected in the nature of their settlement in New York. The newly arrived discovered a residential pattern already in existence; and, in distributing themselves through the city, largely accepted the conditions imposed by that pattern, complicated, however, by the rise in total population and the consequent increase in density of residence.

As earlier, speculators in real estate found it advantageous to allow marginal properties to deteriorate. The rise in the level of taxation made investment in such holdings preferable to that in vacant land so long as there was enough rental income to cover current charges. There was consequently still a rapid change in the character of neighborhoods. Within that context, in general, a combination of income and ethnic factors dictated the choice of a domicile. The poorest elements in the population had the least mobility and were confined to the center of the city; the wealthier moved outward, in a direction shaped by ethnic considerations.[62]

There was, it was true, a large floating population of unaffiliated individuals and families. Such men and women, whatever their origin, had dissolved their ties with the ethnic group; and they selected their homes primarily on the basis of personal convenience and income. They took advantage of opportunities for anonymity supplied by the large and growing number of boarding houses and apartments in districts like Greenwich Village; and their number was constantly being replenished by members of the second generation who wished to escape their immigrant affiliations. Yet in a sense even these people constituted a group for whom ethnic considerations had an import, although a negative one. In avoiding Irish, Jewish, or German neighborhoods, they constituted themselves a group of the unaffiliated.

For most New Yorkers, ethnic affiliation remained significant to the third generation and beyond. Even in the 1920's, the great-grandchildren of the German or Irish immigrants of the 1830's or 1840's and the great-great-grandchildren of the Yankees of 1800 still had meaningful ties to the groups of their ancestors. Those ties established the character of the group's identification. The wish to live close to people of similar backgrounds was fed by the desire to share common religious and cultural resources; and the ability to shop in familiar stores and to attend a familiar church strengthened ethnic links and established the character of a neighborhood whether that extended over one block or many. Children who grew up within the same environment tended to marry within the group so that the ethnic ties passed from generation to generation; and, even when circumstances compelled a group to change its residence, those ties continued to influence the direction of their movement.[63]

The developing lines of settlement can therefore best be traced in ethnic terms. The descendants of the original settlers were by the 1880's usually identified as Anglo-Saxons, a term defined by contrast with the immigrants of the period after 1820. The common element that held this group together was its Protestantism and the absence of any other affiliation. It included not only the old Dutch and English families, but also the New Englanders and Quakers of the first half of the nineteenth century and occasional Scots, English, Welsh, and even Germans and Frenchmen who arrived later but attached themselves to it.

The poor and unsuccessful in this group were generally lost in characterless enclaves scattered throughout the city, in part of the West Side, of Greenwich Village, in Brooklyn, and later in Queens, where they were surrounded by communities of the foreign-born. The very poorest were left behind, immobilized by their failure, and swamped beneath the successive waves of immigrants. In the notorious "Big Flat" tenement on Mott Street, for instance, lived 478 residents, of whom 368 were Jews and 31 Italians, who were just entering the neighborhood. But there were also 31 Irish, 30 Germans, and 4 natives, a kind of sediment left behind when their groups departed. However, among the Anglo-Saxons, these were a small minority as compared with the families of wealth or of moderate incomes.[64]

The very wealthiest segments of this group were able to maintain a high degree of freedom of choice as to residence. They entrenched themselves in the good sections of Greenwich Village and built their town houses up the East Side of Manhattan with Fifth Avenue and Central Park providing a protective barrier against the fringe of unwelcome neighbors. They could take refuge also in country estates scattered across the two hundred miles between Southampton, Long Island, and Tuxedo Park—this in addition to vacation homes and resorts more remote still.

The less wealthy, although by no means poor, were not so fortunate. Such people were small proprietors or held managerial, clerical, and professional positions. But they were anxious to make the most of their incomes and wished, above all, to preserve their status, threatened by contact with the foreigners. The desire to do so was not merely a matter of sentiment. Identification with good family, neighborhood, churches, schools, and societies could open valuable opportunities for mobility upward for themselves and their children. The wrong identifications could create serious obstacles.

That anxiety was the dynamic element in their situation. These people could not remain where they were when their neighborhoods were threatened. As immigrants moved in, the Protestant churches found their Sunday schools, attendance at services, and membership dwindling so that the costs for those who remained mounted astronomically.[65] The old shops lost patronage and the public schools changed in character. Anyone who stayed was engulfed in a new ethnic community. It was therefore essential to move and wisest to do so at the first hint of a change.[66]

Hence the persistent concern about desirable places of residence. The boarding house and hotel life of the earlier period was no longer feasible except for the newly married, for the costs rose rapidly after the Civil War. Yet the range of permissible choices for an independent household was most limited. Those who were willing to live in apartments built in the 1880's and 1890's after the French fashion could find space on the upper West Side of Manhattan. The area above 59th Street had still been mostly vacant in 1881.[67] It was to fill up quickly with such inhabitants in the next two decades.[68]

But the apartment house was slow to take hold and at first received only those who had no alternative. "The Stuyvesant," built in 1869, had been regarded with distrust; and a persistent prejudice nagged most people with aspirations toward respectable status in the conviction that they must be property owners and live in single-family dwellings, whatever the cost. The one-family house and garden—though it be a plot but 20 x 100—became a symbol of their Americanism and drove them steadily outward toward the suburban fringes of the city.

It was impossible to hold on to space of this sort near the center. The rapid spread of cheap transit facilities in Manhattan and the rise in passenger volume were signs of the intrusion throughout the island of the masses of the poor willing to accept high-density housing. In 1890 the good single-family house survived only in the northernmost reaches of Manhattan and on the edge of Brooklyn. Those who sought such residences then had to look outward to Flatbush, Flatlands, Bensonhurst, Queens, the Bronx, and New Jersey where promoters were converting farms into lots. For those who could afford the time and the carfare, these areas were brought within reach of the central city by a network of trolley lines and commuting railways; yet their remoteness and expense isolated them from the poor.[69]

Nonetheless, these comfortable neighborhoods of rustic villas and cottages proved unstable. Already in the 1890's with the extension of elevated rapid transit to some peripheral areas, new groups intruded. Lines of row houses with relatively cheap flats advanced into Harlem. In the same decade the old residents began to flee from Greenwich Village, not to return until the rehabilitation of the area after 1915.[70] After 1900 the subway began to bring many outlying regions within uncomfortable, cheap, and easy access; in 1924 it was carrying 4,000,000 riders a day.

Those who could, therefore, fled to districts still farther away, by the Hudson tubes opened in 1904 to New Jersey, by the Queensborough Bridge opened in 1910 to Queens, and by railway and automobile to Westchester and Long Island. By 1928 more than a quarter of a million persons commuted daily by railroad. Others struggled to stay on, protecting the integrity of their neighborhoods by restrictive covenants and property owners' associations to keep away outsiders. These "Old Americans" therefore were sensitive to every pressure on their living space.[71]

That pressure came from the fact that the population was not only expanding, but expanding through the growth of ethnic groups with whom the Anglo-Saxons were unwilling to be identified. For none of the immigrants remained stable. The conditions of their adjustment early set them in motion; from 1870 onward the Irish and Germans were dynamically moving groups.

By then the least prosperous had been ruthlessly eliminated; that was the effect of the murderous mortality rates of the 1850's. The rest achieved some degree of stratification. Some remained unskilled laborers. They stayed either downtown or in the middle West Side, beyond Eighth Avenue and between 23rd and 59th Streets, where the other shanty towns were transformed into Hell's Kitchen, a teeming neighborhood that housed laborers from the docks and from the nearby piano, carpet, and soap factories, and also a good part of the city's vice and crime.[72]

But the Irishmen and Germans who rose in the world to become skilled workingmen or clerks or proprietors and the second generation, which grew ever larger and more important, wished to break away and to acquire the superior status commensurate with their rise. Such people sought to imitate the way of life of the Anglo-Saxons. Like the latter they also sought to avoid identification with the still newer immigrant greenhorns. They, and each successive group after them, found themselves drawn into a pattern of Americanization that demanded of them a complex of culture changes, in habits and tastes, in family size and language, and also in standards of housing. The Irish and Germans were, therefore, to a certain degree competitors with the old Americans for the better living places in the city; and since they moved in groups the competition was not simply one of individuals but of communities.[73]

Although very fortunate individuals in these groups were able to seek residences similar in style to the wealthy Anglo-Saxons, the great mass occupied positions in the lower middle class and in the working class; and they had difficulty in finding respectable, desirable housing.

The Irish and Germans had some advantages, however. While they too longed for the one-family house, even the two-family dwelling or the good flat was an advance for which they were willing to pay more than their rivals. In this regard there were significant differences between the Irish and the Germans. Among the latter were a larger percentage of artisans and merchants, children of immigrants of the period before 1850, who provided leadership and raised the level of the whole group. Furthermore, religion was a more cohesive factor among the Irish than among the Germans. The Protestantism of the latter gave them a point of contact with the Anglo-Saxons that the Irish lacked. Significantly, German Catholics were sometimes driven to identification with the Irish.

From the census statistics, the Irish appear to be scattered everywhere throughout the city. But that is to some extent a reflection of the fact that many were servants in the households of Yankees. Actually, there was a good deal of concentration. In the 1880's and 1890's some of the Irish still struggled to maintain the better neighborhoods on the Lower East Side and succeeded in doing so on isolated blocks. Others moved into Greenwich Village and up the West Side toward Washington Heights and toward the Bronx. From the nuclei of Irishtown settlements around Jay Street and elsewhere in Brooklyn, they drifted southward toward the Bay Ridge section. Other clusters of them had also appeared around the docks and factories where they worked on the Jersey side of the river.

The Germans appeared to be still more concentrated, but that may be due to the fact that there were fewer servants among them. In 1890, most of the group still lived on the East Side north of Rivington Street. They moved in two distinct columns from this original center of settlement. To the north they were at first blocked off by the high price area of Murray Hill and Grand Central. Skirting that, they pre-empted the Yorkville region immediately above it which acquired a distinctive Teutonic character. Meanwhile others of them went across the East River bridges to the boroughs of Brooklyn and Queens, where they established a string of settlements that straggled on toward Bushwick and Ridgewood. Still others established stable communities in Newark, Irvington, and other New Jersey towns.[74]

Both the Irish and the Germans were impelled to move by pressure from the still newer immigrant groups who poured into the original areas of settlement. The Italians, in the beginning, occupied the least desirable blocks of the old East Side. They lived at first in rear tenements behind the Irish, then took over entire districts as their predecessors fled. They clustered west of the Bowery around Mulberry Bend, the site of the old Collect Pond, now filled in, but still a noxious place of residence.[75] The East European Jews had been settled earlier in the fourth and sixth wards around Park Row and Baxter Street. But they shifted after 1870 and occupied a region of the East Side somewhat to the north of the Italians and east of the Bowery, moving into houses then being vacated by the Germans. Both districts were transformed by the new style tenements in the 1890's to hold a far larger population than ever before.[76]

Other smaller groups also located themselves in enclaves in the vicinity. By the turn of the century, there were distinct colonies of Orientals in Chinatown, of Greeks in Hell's Kitchen, of French and Lithuanians in Greenwich Village, of Bohemians along the East River between 59th Street and 76th Street, of Poles and Ruthenians in Jersey City, and of Syrians on lower Washington Street.[77]

Within a relatively short period the new immigrants too began to seek better quarters. In many cases, it was only a year or two before they moved, pulled by the attractions of improved housing and pushed by pressure from still newer arrivals. They were, however, forced to pick their way across the face of the city among the spaces taken by rivals who were there first. They were aided by the fact that they showed a greater willingness than the older residents to accept multiple-family housing.

The Jews were quickest to move. They had the advantage of previous skills and therefore the highest rate of occupational mobility. That put them most promptly in the position to quit the old East Side, which was nevertheless replenished by newcomers as long as immigration persisted. Only after World War I did the population of the district decline.

By 1900 a substantial number of Jews had already departed and the volume of those who joined the exodus grew continually. In that year a few of them were already scattered east of Fifth Avenue between 40th Street and 86th Street. But it was difficult for most of those who wished to abandon the East Side to move directly to the north, for there they were blocked by people with some power of resistance. The Jews had to skip over the old American neighborhoods on the upper East Side and over German Yorkville before proceeding first to Harlem and thence across the river to the Bronx. The Williamsburgh Bridge opened another line of settlement and took other Jews into Williamsburgh in Brooklyn and thence along the lines of the rapid transit system to relatively empty spaces in Borough Park and Brownsville.[78]

The experience of the Italians was similar, although it proceeded at a somewhat slower pace, and more areas were therefore blocked off by the time their move began. One group broke westward into districts of Greenwich Village formerly inhabited by Germans and Irish. Another occupied a section of Harlem to the east of that held by the Jews; in 1900 there was already a "Little Italy" at 110th Street. Other colonies were planted in Fordham Road in the Bronx, and in the Bushwick and Fourth Avenue districts of Brooklyn. Those more prosperous still migrated first to Long Island City, Flushing, Corona, and Astoria, and thence into blocks of Borough Park and Bensonhurst in Brooklyn. By 1928 there were some twenty communities in the city, the population of which was 50 to 90 per cent Italian, often concentrated in terms of province of origin.[79]

Thus, the pattern of movement was the product of a complex of forces. Newly arriving groups occupied the cheapest and least desirable residential sections. That was why the population of the East Side, and of Manhattan generally, grew rapidly so long as immigrants flowed into the city. Both began to decline after 1914 when the flow slackened.[80]

The constant pressure from newcomers displaced older elements in the population who moved in a direction determined by the ability of each group to find available space. That in turn was conditioned by several factors. Duration of settlement generally increased mobility. As the years passed and a family aged, as its children married and as it ceased to take in boarders, its diminishing needs and increasing means opened even wider ranges of choice to it. Small groups, however, were usually less mobile than large ones and had to cling together despite the emergence of important internal differences. Hostile relations along the borders of a district made a long move preferable to a contiguous spread. A quick improvement in occupational status supplied the means of frequent change in residence. The development of the rapid transit system allowed men to sacrifice the convenience of closeness to their jobs for the sake of homes in better neighborhoods. Such varied influences shaped the kaleidoscopic character of the city's residential pattern. The fact, however, that the whole city was expanding with great rapidity in the half-century after 1870 gave all the groups within it some space for maneuver.[81]

The patterns of employment and the character of the settlement profoundly influenced the adjustment of both the new and the old residents to the urban problems of a growing metropolis. The physical difficulties alone were of enormous magnitude and the men who coped with them found few precedents of assistance. Despite endless experiment the problem of finding decent working-class housing was never solved. In districts like the East Side the available space did not grow as rapidly as the population, and overcrowding was a constant source of deterioration and of reflected disorders in sanitation and health. Dirty crowded streets lined with dirty crowded tenements were a poor setting for urban life.[82]

Through the period, therefore, complaints continued about pauperism, crime, juvenile delinquency, disease, and the other evils of the slums, often associating those disorders with immigration.[83] There may well have been some increase in the rate of delinquency, although perceptive contemporary observers were by no means sure even of that and precise measurements are difficult.[84] But in any case the monotony of these complaints, which were already being sounded in the early nineteenth century and are still being heard, obscures the really distinctive features of the problem.

Three different phenomena were involved in the delinquency of this period. The first was the disorder produced by the process of moving an enormous number of people quickly into a limited space. The difficulty of doing so was compounded by the fact that the newcomers lacked experience with urban living and were strangers in the United States. The results were the poor housing of the slums and the attendant high rates of disease and mortality. Given the nature of urban growth in these years, these difficulties were perhaps unavoidable. Yet there was measurable progress in dealing with them; and when the tide of immigration slackened and the rate of population increase fell, after 1920, a prospect of solution came within sight.

Failures in government were a second source of delinquency. New York was slow to adapt to new needs the forms of local government inherited from a rural past; and the result was often a breakdown in the protection of its residents against disorder. Occasional efforts at reform produced a temporary difference in cleaner streets and less corrupt police. Similarly, an awakening to the nature of the problem led to a steady lowering of the incidence of tuberculosis in the city after the turn of the century. But such spasmodic improvements did not offset the general atmosphere of disorderliness. While that may not have produced criminal impulses within the individual, it certainly accounted for the pervasive place of criminality in the society. It helped confuse standards of behavior to an extent that disoriented all those whose situation was precarious.[85]

Finally, some problems were rooted in failures of personal adjustment. The high rates of intemperance, prostitution, pauperism, gambling, criminality, and juvenile delinquency could not be ascribed simply to external conditions.[86] These were also the results of the destruction of old habits and of the shocking effects of new conditions. The disruption of family ties and the dissolution of the authority of accepted values unsettled the norms of personal behavior and left the individual confused and therefore vulnerable at moments of crisis.[87] That was why the second generation was in a particularly precarious situation. Compelled to devise their own standards, its members often found those in conflict with the rules of established society, so that street sports and gang activity verged almost imperceptibly over into crime and vice.[88]

The degree of susceptibility to one or another of these disorders varied from ethnic group to ethnic group, although none was altogether free of them.[89] The differences in order reflected differences in the point of breakdown, determined by cultural experience. Under comparable pressure, for instance, the collapse of an Irishman would more often take the form of intemperance than would that of an Italian.[90] More generally, it is possible only to establish a vague inverse relation between the rate of delinquency and the capacity of the group to make a favorable economic and social adjustment to the new conditions of life in New York.

Yet the personal tension was rarely transmuted into overt intergroup conflict. Significant expressions of prejudice extended from the street warfare of boys' gangs to the exclusionary practices of select clubs.[91] The pressure of limited housing created bad feelings, particularly in marginal or transitional neighborhoods. But the very high degree of heterogeneity demanded an accommodation of some sort; and the very multiplicity of groups in the city prevented any clear-cut alignments, such as might decisively isolate any single sector of the population. As a result, New Yorkers came to feel a sense of pride in the cosmopolitan character of their city.

"New York," said a distinguished newspaper editor, "has a more stupendous problem than any city on this 'terrestrial sphere' has ever had before. It has the largest and most varied 'agglomeration of mankind,' brought together not by ancestral predestination, but almost wholly by personal or parental choice; it has probably the most varied and considerable industries of hand and machine ever brought into one neighborhood since the sons of Lamech began to manufacture things; and it is the greatest port and center of communication, transportation, and exchange, by water, land and air, on the face of the planet." [92]

Thus the city's diversity was generally regarded as a source of strength rather than of weakness. Politics, the character of communal organization and of its leadership, and the metropolitan context together created conditions favorable to effective controls.

New York politics provided a means of adjustment rather than a source of conflict as it did in other cities like Boston. Varied groups identified themselves with one party or another, as the Irish did with the Democrats. But almost everyone realized that no single group was numerous enough either to hold power alone or to think only of its own interests. Occasionally nationalists attempted to give primacy to their particular objectives as when Patrick Ford of the *Irish World* and John Devoy of the *Irish Nation* in 1884 tried to swing the Irish vote to the Republican Blaine. Their failure in the face of the opposition of the professional politicians showed where power really rested.[93]

To secure control it was necessary to attract support from a variety of groups, a necessity the logic of which Tammany Hall understood with particular clarity. Charles Murphy, the Irish leader after the turn of the century, thus made it a point to keep close ties to the Jews and the Germans and later to the Italians. The local club faithfully reflected the composition of its neighborhood; and, while often one ethnic group predominated among its membership, it nevertheless made room for every bloc of potential voters. Al Smith, the characteristic hero of the city in the last decade of this period, again and again recognized the importance of harmony among the diverse elements of the population.[94]

Voluntary associations, to operate in the broad areas of social action left to nongovernmental agencies, had already appeared before the Civil War. After 1870 they grew more numerous and more important; and they were integrated into coherent communal organizations. They too eased many of the problems of intergroup adjustment.

The increase in the size and in the number of the immigrant groups made possible a greater diversity in the character of their associations. For a long time there had been societies to represent each of the linguistic and religious sectors of the population—Irish, German, Jewish, and the like. Now these multiplied to make room for many more particular differences, in local origin, in religious affiliation, in time of emigration, and in social and economic status. Jewish *landsmannschaften,* Irish and Italian provincial societies, and uptown as well as downtown organizations reflected the multiplicity of types now possible. As a result, they served their social and cultural functions more effectively.[95] The church remained a cohesive social as well as religious organization, but now there was variety in point of view, so that there were Italian as well as Irish Catholic churches, East European as well as German synagogues.[96] By the same token, the theater flourished for several different audiences on different levels.[97] And, finally, the press became an important instrument of social expression.[98]

The development of fully functioning ethnic communities served those who needed help with specific problems and relieved the state of part of the burden of welfare work. It also furnished the individual with a medium through which he could understand the difficulties of the strange society around him and relate himself meaningfully to it. The ethnic community supplied its members with norms and values and with the direction of an elite leadership. It not only assisted them in dealing with their own problems and in adjusting to the conditions of American life, but also gave them a pattern of acceptable forms of action and of expression, connected with the forms of the larger society about them, but integrated in a context intelligible in their own lives.[99]

The communal leadership of these years was somewhat different from that of the earlier part of the century. The normal pattern still emphasized the high rank of the successful businessman. But men of wealth were less likely than earlier to take a direct part in the management of communal affairs. They more often acted through intermediaries, particularly through such professionals as the lawyers. This pattern was repeated in most ethnic groups, with some variations arising out of special circumstances. Among the Jews, for instance, one segment of the community looked for leadership to the lawyers and another to functionaries of the labor unions. Among the Irish, for whom the church and politics were the most important channels of social advance, businessmen were less consequential than the politicians and clergymen. But these were differences of degree. In all groups, those who had made good in "American" terms were models to be emulated; and their ability to succeed testified to the possibility of adjustment by the whole group.[100]

Two elements in the social context were particularly important in easing the process of adjustment. The rapid expansion of the city and of its population made room for newcomers and also steadily raised real estate values which made moving less painful. And the extension of the residential area was accompanied by an extension of public transportation. As a result, almost every element in the population enjoyed the mobility to seek more desirable houses. Although the wealthy moved first, people with lower incomes in time also were able to attain some degree of relative improvement. The goal of a decent setting for family life therefore seemed attainable and worth working for. Whether a given individual reached it or not, the hope of it gave some stability and purpose to his toil.

A significant test of the success of the adjustment came during World War I. The city remained relatively untouched by the xenophobia and the subsequent red scare that swept through the rest of the country. The large German-American population was severely tested by the strain on its loyalties and that may have weakened somewhat its determination to maintain its identity after 1920. But it did not suffer the abuse visited on Americans of German descent elsewhere. The tradition of cosmopolitanism preserved New York from the disorder of group conflict.[101]

Shortly after the end of the war, however, forces generated outside the city brought immigration to an end. Significantly, the bitterness and hatred that contributed to the postwar antiforeign feeling were hardly evident in the city itself. The foreigners had not antagonized the people who lived with them; but they had earned the hostility of the rural folk of the West and the South who had little direct contact with the urban population.

Those elements were powerful enough to secure enactment of the immigration legislation of 1921 and 1924 which effectively cut off the flow of newcomers from Europe. After 1924, only a trickle moved into the country; and the onset of the depression of 1929 made the revival of the old kind of immigration unlikely. Thereafter, the need for the type of labor the immigrants had supplied would have to be met from sources not covered by the immigration law—from within the United States and its territorial possessions.[102]

3

The Newest Immigrants

After 1930, New York City continued to grow, although at a moderating pace. The population of the municipality reached its peak shortly after 1950. The special census of 1957 for the first time revealed a decline; in seven years, the city had suffered a loss of some 1.2 per cent. In that interval, a decline of some 416,000 in the number of whites had more than offset a rise of some 320,000 in the number of nonwhites.[1]

The population figures for the area contained within the political limits of New York, however, no longer mirror the extent of its expansion—any more than those for Manhattan alone did after 1900. Increasingly, the city has become integrated into the metropolitan region of which it is the center; and the operations of ponderous social and cultural forces have combined to locate an increasingly larger part of its inhabitants on its outskirts rather than in its inner core.

The measurements of population growth are therefore most meaningfully viewed in these larger terms. The New York metropolitan region has increased in number of inhabitants to somewhat over fifteen million. Whatever out-migration has occurred from the area in the past two decades has been more than offset by natural increase through excess of births over deaths and by the entry of newcomers from outside the region. It is safe to predict that, however the population will be distributed inside it, the metropolitan area as a whole will continue to grow. Estimates of its population by 1975 range as high as twenty million.[2]

The natural increase by the excess of births over deaths has played a larger part in recent than in past growth. The mortality rate has fallen steadily; and the birth rate, after sinking to a low in the 1930's, began to rise after 1940, as it did elsewhere in the United States. There seems no reason to anticipate a marked reversal of those trends in the near future. Indeed, changing marriage patterns foreshadow further increases of this sort.[3]

The ethnic groups already established in New York before 1930 continued to retain their identity, although it was no longer possible to count the number of their members with any degree of precision. As the first and second generations died out and were replaced by a third and fourth generation, the foreign-born and the children of the foreign-born ceased to make a significant appearance in the census data. The last enumeration which was useful from this point of view was that of 1940.[4] But, even in that census, only the groups which had recently arrived made a significant showing; size was simply an inverse factor of time of arrival. Since 1940 the identification of the membership of various ethnic groups has become more difficult still, as the marks of foreign birth or non-English mother tongue fade with time.[5]

Yet, although these groups no longer make a striking appearance in official enumerations, other evidence indicates that the ties that hold together Jews or Italians or Irish-Americans are still significant. By and large, they reflect the original composition of the population. The character of some groups has changed and there is some loss by intermarriage and by passing, that is, by the unobtrusive movement of individuals from one identification to another. But these shifts have not been of such a magnitude as radically to alter the distribution with which the city was left after the great migrations of the nineteenth century.

The great change in the character of New York's population has not been due to the weakening of the old ethnic groups but rather to a shift in the currents of migration by which their numbers were formerly strengthened. The total decline in the number of foreign-born was the result of the ending of the old immigration. The city has still been the goal of thousands of migrants; but these newcomers have come not from foreign countries but from the United States and its territorial possessions. Trans-Atlantic immigration has played a negligible part in the city's life in the last thirty years.

The onset of the depression in 1929, coming so soon after the enactment of the restrictive quota laws, made the prospect for a revival of European immigration slim indeed. This aspect of New York's history had come decisively to an end.

Not even the crisis precipitated by the rise of German fascism induced the American government to deviate from the new policy. Although expressions of sympathy with the refugees from Hitler's tyranny were sincere and widespread, there was no effort between 1933 and the outbreak of the war to relax the immigration laws in the least. All rescue efforts came within the context of existing legislation. In the twelve years beginning with 1933, somewhat less than a quarter-million refugees arrived in the United States; and they did so within the established quotas and in the face of the most stringent application of the restrictive regulations. Some 70 per cent of these newcomers were Jews; the remainder were non-Aryans by Nazi definitions or liberal enemies of the Third Reich.[6]

A substantial number of those who entered the country chose to stay in New York. This was by far the largest port of entry; here were found the communal services that eased the problems of settlement; and here was a cosmopolitan atmosphere attractive to the foreign-born. Above all, it was easier here to find employment that utilized the skill and capital they brought with them.

A substantial number of these newcomers (more than 40 per cent) were businessmen and professional people; these were the groups most likely to possess the means of effecting an escape from Europe. They thus differed significantly from the immigrants of the nineteenth century. Once they surmounted the initial problems of language and employment, they faced few problems of adjustment. Their incomes permitted them a good deal of choice as to residence, although many settled in a rather large community on the upper

West Side. Delinquency, in the old terms, was not a source of difficulty.

After the war, the displaced persons renewed the challenge to American immigration policy. The forces entrenched in support of restriction did not yield. But they were compelled to acquiesce in temporary lowering of the bars for special purposes. The Displaced Persons and Refugee Relief acts of 1948 and 1953 opened the gates to some half-million newcomers; and 38,000 Hungarians squeezed in after the collapse of the revolution of 1956. Nonquota, family, and western hemisphere admittals raised the total for the United States between 1946 and 1957 to 2,600,000.[7]

Of the displaced persons and refugees, about one-quarter made their way to New York City. This was a much more miscellaneous group than the German refugees. It was composed of distinct and widely scattered clusters of population. The fewness of their numbers and the aid they received in resettlement furthered the process of their economic and social adjustment. Arriving as they did in a period of manpower shortage, and sustained by very general communal sympathy, they faced relatively few difficulties in settlement.[8]

Far greater problems were created in the same period by the migration of two large groups of American citizens. The two world wars stimulated interstate and interregional migration and significantly altered their character. This was no longer a flow primarily from east to west, with land the magnet. It was above all a movement toward new industrial centers with the South the greatest loser and the Pacific and north central states the great gainers. But for two groups involved in these migrations, New York became an important destination. The American Negroes and Puerto Ricans paradoxically approached more closely in their experience to the pattern earlier set by Europeans than did the refugee foreigners.[9]

The Negro community in New York was old and well established at the beginning of the twentieth century. It had grown moderately in size since the Civil War. A declining fertility rate, although higher than that of the native white, was far lower than that of the foreign-born. The excess of females in the group and its age distribution indicated a further natural increase in size, but at a more moderate rate. In 1900 the Negroes in the city numbered 60,000, of whom about 18,000 resided in Brooklyn and 36,000 in Manhattan. But the percentage of colored people in the total population had actually fallen so that their importance as a factor in the city seemed to have been diminishing rather than increasing.[10]

The Negroes had made considerable progress in the three decades between 1870 and 1900. Profiting from some abolitionist sympathy in the city and from certain strategic opportunities for advancement, they had earned a minor but secure economic position in the service trades of the city. There were few unskilled laborers among them, so that they did not have to compete for factory jobs against the hordes of poor immigrants. Instead, the colored people had developed the skills that made them prominent in various service occupations. They were barbers, waiters, caterers, and skilled artisans. They also had a small leadership of professional and businessmen. They were, on the whole, therefore, better off than the mass of recent white immigrants. They had shown some ability to organize, and political activity earned municipal jobs for a few of them.[11]

They nevertheless led a narrow, self-contained social life. Although the white schools were opened to them in 1873, they still suffered from discrimination, particularly when they tried to break out of the limited circle of occupations open to them. Toward the end of the nineteenth century, for instance, the organized white carpenters, bricklayers, and plasterers successfully resisted the effort of black workers to enter those trades. Such tensions no doubt contributed to the race riot that flared up in 1900. Despite such handicaps, given the fewness of their numbers, the colored people seemed to be escaping from some of the worst forms of segregation, although within a restricted scope of activity. Certainly the patterns of Jim Crow etiquette and behavior never took hold in the city; nor did the ever-present threat of violence characteristic of the South.[12]

Their situation changed shortly thereafter. In the next two decades two streams of Negro immigration converged upon the city and changed the lot of all its colored people.

The first took form within the southern United States. In the former slave states the long-drawn-out process of depriving the Negroes of the fruits of their freedom had now reached its culmination in their total subordination. Law and custom excluded the black man from the ballot box, from desirable employment, and from equal opportunities for education. The prospects for improvement through remaining where they were seemed dim indeed; and the more adventuresome began to migrate away from the South. In the first three decades after emancipation, the movement was predominantly westward. But, thereafter, the Negroes who sought new homes turned ever more frequently to the North, many of them to New York.[13] In 1910 that city's Negro population had mounted to 91,709, an increase due largely to migration from the South. About 30,000 more lived in the Region's outer towns. At that date, only Washington among American cities held more Negroes; and, with its suburbs, New York held the largest urban Negro population in the United States.[14]

The newcomers of the years down to 1910 were drawn mostly from the closer states of the upper South—Virginia, North Carolina, and Maryland. They were attracted by the prospect of higher wages and better working conditions and also by the freedom from the fear of actual violence that still enveloped them below the Mason-Dixon Line.[15] But after 1915 the desire to migrate penetrated to the deep South also. In the hard times when the boll weevil hit the cotton crop thousands of them began a trek to the northern cities where the word was that there were jobs for them.

The fact that the jobs actually were waiting for them added a pull to the push of southern conditions. The precipitate decline in the volume of European immigration after 1917 created a demand for unskilled manpower in northern industries. The places no longer being held by Italians and Slavs, kept at home by the war, were now to be filled from the one domestic source of cheap labor—the southern Negroes. The main body of these immigrants moved toward the

Middle West, which was closest to the deep South and which was passing through a boom in heavy industry. But a substantial number of them came to New York.

There they were joined by a somewhat smaller group of newcomers from the British West Indies. A few colored people from the Caribbean had come to New York earlier, but before 1900 their numbers had grown slowly. Then came a sharp increase. On the islands, too, a rising population and restricted opportunities generated discontent which pushed many Negroes away. Migration to the mainland rose in the decade after 1900; in 1910 there were fully 10,000 West Indians in New York, one-fourth of all those in the United States.[16]

For such people too, the vacant spaces left by the end of European immigration created a sense of opportunity. The number who left Jamaica, Barbados, and the other islands rose steadily; and this migration was pre-eminently directed toward New York, which was tied to the West Indies by shipping links that were not severed during the war. In 1940, almost 50,000 of them were residents of the city.

As a result of immigration from both sources, the number of Negroes in the city had risen to 150,000 in 1920; and it continued to grow even more rapidly in the next decade. By 1930, the Negro population had climbed to 327,000, most of it concentrated in Harlem but also sprinkled throughout the other boroughs. There were then also sizable groups in New Jersey, Westchester, and Long Island.[17]

The movement slackened somewhat in the 1930's. The restriction of economic opportunity during the depression slowed the flow of Negroes to the city; and there seems actually to have been some return migration. The charge occasionally made at the time that they continued to come north to live off relief is unsubstantiated. In a period of mass unemployment even the most miserable among these people seemed unwilling to move, preferring to accept known miseries rather than to confront unknown dangers.

The migration out of the South resumed, however, as the war approached. The manpower shortage that then developed persisted for more than a decade after the peace. The number of newcomers from the South remained high. On the other hand, migration to the city from the West Indies became less important, particularly after the McCarran-Walter Act imposed a quota restriction upon the British West Indian Negroes for the first time. But the southern migration was large enough to keep the total colored population of the city rising steadily. By 1950, there were fully 1,146,000 in the seventeen-county metropolitan area as defined by the Census Bureau, over 800,000 of them in New York City. The rate of increase since then has remained rapid, both in the central city, where more than a million Negroes now form one-eighth of the total population, and in the outlying region. The presence of these Negroes created an increasingly difficult problem as they came to constitute a larger and larger percentage of its labor force and of its citizenry.[18]

One other substantial group appeared in the city after World War I. The Puerto Ricans were American citizens to whom the immigration laws did not apply. Like the Negroes, they were set in motion by a combination of forces which thrust them away from their island home and at the same time attracted them to New York City.[19]

Puerto Rico's central problem since its annexation to the United States has been overpopulation. A birth rate that was always high and a lower mortality rate that has been declining steadily since 1930 have combined to more than double the population of the island in a half-century. Not until after 1950 did the birth rate sink perceptibly below the level of 40 per thousand. But even that yielded a substantial excess over deaths and led to a population increase of consistently more than 20 per thousand in the last two decades. This was an increase the simple agricultural economy could not absorb. The population per square mile rose steadily from 280 in 1900 to 546 in 1940 to 645 in 1950. In 1935 the island held but 0.79 improved acres per capita; and agricultural improvements since then have not kept pace with the staggering growth in numbers.[20]

The result was a surplus of laborers, often without land or with holdings too small to sustain them. Efforts at induced industrialization and at birth control showed encouraging signs of progress, particularly after 1940. But they did not provide the means for utilizing or liquidating the surplus.

The quest for economic opportunity was the dynamic element that drove great numbers of these people to migration. The jíbaro without means tended first to make his way to the island's chief city, San Juan, the population of which rose steadily. There he fell into a large pool of unskilled labor working for low wages, which his women supplemented with needlework. Unemployment was chronic and seasonally rose to alarmingly high levels. And, while the unemployed were themselves immobilized by their poverty, the pressure of a labor surplus created among those with some means and ambition a pool of Puerto Ricans available for emigration.[21]

The opportunity to come to the mainland was enlarged by the postwar immigration laws which virtually put an end to the admission of Europeans. That left vacant a complex of jobs for unskilled workers partly being filled by Negroes but for which Puerto Ricans could also compete. Immigration started slowly in the 1920's but gained steadily through the decade, although never exceeding 9,000 in any year. But predictions were then already being made that 400,000 Puerto Ricans would come to the United States in the next decade. The shipping lines which tied the island to the mainland had their terminus in New York, so that the bulk of the newcomers landed in the city and stayed there.[22]

During the depression, however, the movement slowed down; in some years the number of departures actually exceeded the number of arrivals. In the 1930's, nevertheless, the basis was being established, in Puerto Rico and in New York, for the more extensive migration that was to follow. The island was hard-hit economically. A large part of the population fell on relief and the pool of potential emigrants grew steadily larger. Meanwhile, those already in New York were establishing a bridgehead that would receive later arrivals.[23]

The movement of Puerto Ricans to the mainland resumed when the war restored the demand for manpower. The renewal of that

flow coincided with and was stimulated by a radical change in transportation—the establishment of regular air service between San Juan
and New York. The airplane was not only speedier than and as
cheap as the steamship, but, in addition, it could accommodate far
larger numbers and it made the trip less burdensome. For as little as
fifty dollars in six hours of flight a Puerto Rican could find his way
to the opportunities of the mainland and be abundantly repaid by its
relatively higher wages.[24]

Since the shortage of manpower persisted after the war the immigration remained heavy. The volume of entrants grew steadily
except in the brief periods of recession. The return migration was
always substantial. But the annual net intake was in the vicinity of
40,000, fluctuating from year to year with the state of the American
economy. Well over half a million arrived in the United States between 1941 and 1956. With their native-born children they formed a
population of considerably more than 700,000.[25]

The number of Puerto Ricans permanently domiciled in New
York City also grew. The connection by air, like that by sea, was
with New York which became the initial point of reception. The
percentage of the new arrivals who remained there was always large.
But it tended to fall somewhat between 1920 and 1940 and, after a
sharp rise in the 1940's, declined again after 1950.[26] The metropolis
was attractive because it already contained a substantial nucleus of
Puerto Ricans, because it could use their labor, and because it had
the reputation of comparative freedom from prejudice and discrimination.[27] Efforts to distribute them to other labor markets had some
effect. More than 160,000 ultimately settled outside New York.[28] But
the advantages of the city remained compelling for a decisive majority. More than 400,000 became residents; with their native children
they now form a group of somewhat more than 600,000.[29] (There is
also a much smaller contingent of other Latin-Americans, variously
referred to as "Cubans" and "Spanish.")

Together the Negroes and Puerto Ricans in the metropolitan
region number about 2,000,000, an increase in little more than a

quarter-century of almost 250 per cent. This is thus a migration comparable in scope to that of the Irish and Germans between 1840 and 1860 and of the Jews and Italians, 1890–1915.

The prospects for continued immigration in the future are not difficult to assess. It may be said categorically that large-scale immigration from Europe is not in the foreseeable future likely to reappear as a factor influencing the population of metropolitan New York. The quota system is an effective barrier that shuts out newcomers from the lands most likely to produce them. But even if, as is possible, there should before long be some significant modification in the statutes, the high cost of migration now and restrictions within the European countries themselves will keep the flow from attaining the old levels. Barring some major catastrophe it is unlikely that substantial numbers of Europeans will again migrate to the United States. New York will not therefore in the future be able to draw upon this source for additions to its population.

The factors that will in the future condition the volume of Negro and Puerto Rican immigration are more complex and will be less readily controlled than was the movement of foreigners. The city and the state have only limited power to regulate the entrance within their borders of newcomers; and those powers are particularly slim when it comes to American citizens, as California discovered when it tried to deny admission to the "Okies" in the 1930's. Unskilled labor furthermore is more fluid than skilled and less readily channeled to particular job locations.

In the case of both the Negroes and the Puerto Ricans, conditions at the point of origin will continue to create a substantial reserve of potential migrants. But the movement that might be generated as a result will not necessarily be directed toward New York.

On the basis of past trends, it is possible to predict that the number of Negroes and Puerto Ricans in the metropolitan region will grow by immigration and by natural increase although not as rapidly in the next two decades as in the past two. The increase is not likely to exceed 100 per cent nor is it likely to fall below 50 per cent. A rise in numbers of between 60 and 75 per cent seems most probable. Since the growth in the size of the non-Puerto Rican whites will be smaller, the Negroes and Puerto Ricans then will form between 18 and 20 per cent of the region's population.

The factors that sustain these conclusions are readily summarized. They depend on estimates of both the volume of future immigration and of the magnitude of the natural increase of the two groups.

In Puerto Rico the problem of overpopulation will remain serious for the next generation at least. The island now holds over 2,300,000 people, an increase of more than 30 per cent in the last quarter-century. There is hope of course that the birth rate, which has declined in the last twenty years, will continue to fall and will eventually flatten out. There are indications of a changing ideal of family size and of an increased tolerance and use of birth control devices. These tendencies may actually be stimulated in the future by the rise in income and in level of education with which they are associated. But the dynamics of the life of the extended family and traditional conceptions of the role of husband and wife discountenance the expectation of an early radical change. Futhermore, the large number of young people in the population and the increase in the number of marriages add to the prospect of a continued high birth rate. It is possible that the population of the island may actually double in the next thirty years.[30]

Under those circumstances, the pool of potential emigrants will persist. Although land reform, internal migration, and continued industrialization may raise the capacity of the island to support its people, unemployment is still high and rises with every contraction in the mainland economy.[31] Furthermore, the decline in mortality has been so striking, with a rise in life expectancy at birth from 46 years in 1939–1941 to 61 in the present decade, that the excess of population will remain permanent. That surplus, estimates of which range between 35,000 and 50,000 persons a year, will constitute a pool of future potential migrants. Despite any foreseeable rise in personal incomes many Puerto Ricans in that pool will continue to wish to emigrate. There is an indication that this will be more than a temporary relation in the fact that the proportion of women to men, after remaining abnormally high for many years, since 1950 has leveled off at about parity.[32]

The same is likely to be true in the case of the southern Negroes. The long-term rate of colored population increase has been declining.[33] But changes in agriculture and increasing mechanization are almost certain to continue to displace large numbers of Negroes in the future as in the past. These people, once set in motion, are likely to maintain a high degree of mobility and to seek the best possible job wherever it may be found. In the last decade they have been an important element in the flow of population away from the South, mostly to the Midwest.

Whether the Negroes leave the region or not will depend upon a complex of economic, social, and political factors. Thus far they have not gained directly by the growth of manufacturing in the South. Industrialization has absorbed many displaced white farmers, but few colored ones. It would take a radical reversal of attitudes on the part of employers, unions, and co-workers to make room for the Negroes even if industrial expansion in the South continued at the rate of the fifteen years since the war. It seems far more probable that the economic changes of the next quarter-century will continue to generate a surplus of colored people available for emigration.[34]

The social and political factors likely to operate in the next two decades will also encourage migration. If there is no early and radical improvement in the Negroes' condition, the discrepancy between the South's discrimination and its segregated patterns of living on the one hand, and the relative freedom of the northern industrial centers on the other, will grow greater; and that will increase the attractiveness of every opportunity to move.

It is more likely, however, that there will be progress in the South toward equality of opportunity and condition, however much turmoil will accompany it. But that progress will come slowly and by degrees in one area of social contact after another. In that form, improvement of status will always be accompanied by intergroup tension which will drag from one issue to another as the consequences of genuine equality become clear. The conflict over education will lead to successive conflicts over employment, over voting, over office-holding, and over housing. The resolution of one difficulty will only the more expose those unresolved, until the Negro has gained the genuine equality of opportunity he comes ever more frequently to regard as his due. One can be fairly sure of genuine progress in these matters in the future. But a quarter-century will not be too long to liquidate the tragic heritage of the last three centuries.

In any case the Negro will, for a long time, have to balance as against the hesitance to leave the place of his birth and the fear of a strange new home, the tension and conflict of a society slow and reluctant to accept him as an equal. That will keep the pool of migrants as large in the next quarter-century as it has been in the past four decades.[35]

In both Puerto Rico and the South, therefore, the potential for emigration will remain high in the next twenty-five years. Whether these migrants will actually come to the New York Metropolitan Region, however, is another question. Since these migrants enjoy much greater mobility than any of their predecessors, the answer will depend on whether the city can supply the kinds of jobs which create opportunities. If it does not, they have the alternatives of remaining where they are or of going elsewhere.

In the past century, migration into the New York area has come to correspond ever more directly with fluctuations in the business cycle. As improved communications brought potential immigrants into closer contact with the labor market in the United States, they responded more sensitively to variations in the opportunities for employment. Prosperity pulled them across; in depression the pull slackened and many who had already come returned to their former homes. This has been particularly the case among the Puerto Ricans.[36]

Furthermore, in the future, New York will compete against other labor markets in the United States for both the Negroes and the Puerto Ricans. From the start of large-scale migration, the midwestern industrial cities were more accessible than New York to the

Puerto Rican Migration and United States National Income

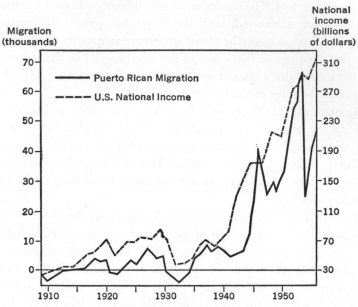

Source: *A Summary in Facts and Figures,* April 1957, p. 15.

Negroes of the deep South. Since the war these people have also found it possible to move in large numbers to the Pacific Coast. In the future, therefore, colored men who wish to leave the South will weigh the advantages of New York against those of Cleveland, Chicago, Detroit, and Los Angeles.

In the past, that was less true of the Puerto Ricans whose settlement was highly concentrated in New York. But the degree of concentration, after mounting to a peak in the middle 1930's, has significantly fallen off after a brief postwar rise. Other centers of settlement have appeared in Chicago, Philadelphia, and lesser industrial towns. While these are still far smaller than that of New York, they have grown rapidly and they have potential importance as nuclei of future expansion. Their residents make relatives and friends back on the island at least aware that there are alternatives to New York. Furthermore, the labor clearing facilities of the United States Employment Service and the Puerto Rican Department of Labor have directed some new arrivals into farm employment. It is therefore likely in the decades to come that the extension of air transportation, the policy of the Puerto Rican government, and greater familiarity with alternative employment centers will give these people a greater range of choice than they have exercised in the past.[37]

In the case of the Negroes, there may also be developing a smaller movement from within the South, as professionally trained and managerial groups in other cities move to the more attractive life of New York, drawn by cultural and social rather than economic reasons. Such a movement will, however, be slight in numbers and will be more than balanced by a countermovement of Negroes trained in New York to special opportunities outside the city.

In general, therefore, immigration is not likely in the future to exercise the determining influence on New York that it did in the past. A pool of potential immigrants will be available if the manpower requirements of the city create the opportunities for it. But it is unlikely to flow in this direction in the absence of such explicit demands.

In-migration is, however, only one of the factors that will determine the future size of these groups in the city. In addition, it is necessary to take into account also their rate of natural increase, the possibilities for out-migration, and the factors that will shape the tenacity of identification of individuals with these groups.

Demographic data, although of limited value in the case of the Puerto Ricans, points to a continued increase of both that group and the Negroes in the New York Metropolitan Region. Both have a high birth rate in the place of their origin; and both bring that with them. While the birth rate shows signs of declining in both groups, it is still higher than that of other elements in New York's population; and it will remain so as long as these people are reluctant to use effective means of limiting the size of their families. Furthermore, the declining mortality of the group will lead to a substantial excess of births over deaths through the next decade even if there is a substantial decline in the birth rate. The rising percentage of Negroes and Puerto Ricans among the city's children already reflects that trend.[38]

There is likely to be some emigration on the part of both groups, although limited to particular sectors of the population. The industrial labor force is not likely to move out. In the absence of cheaper rivals it will probably find conditions in New York more attractive than elsewhere. Even where a differential exists between Negro and Puerto Rican earnings on the one hand, and those of non-Puerto Rican whites on the other, it is smaller in New York than elsewhere. That has made the city attractive to newcomers and will continue to hold them.[39]

Those segments of the labor force which rise into the service trades and occupations are also likely to remain fixed. Insofar as they depend upon a local clientele and face fewer problems of general discrimination in New York than elsewhere, social conditions are likely to bind them to the Region. That is also true of the small business groups. Migration is thus likely to be limited to those who have acquired some skills or professions in the city and find them more useful outside it. But this group will be small in size and will scarcely affect the total structure of the population.

Finally, it seems unlikely that "passing," the loss of identification with the group, will significantly diminish its size. The experience of white Europeans has shown that identification often persists over three or four generations. Yet both the Negroes and the Puerto Ricans are more likely to retain their identity than Europeans for both groups have been vitally affected by the ineradicable complication of color.

In the case of the Negro, color is a recognizable and indelible sign of identification. Furthermore, the predominant American attitude that any degree of color puts an individual within the group prevents its dilution. A single Negro grandparent will tie an individual to the group, as an Irish or Jewish grandparent may not. In any case, in recent years a growing sense of pride in color often leads even those who might pass as marginal whites to prefer to retain their identification with the Negroes. It seems unlikely thus that the group will diminish in size on this account.[40]

The situation of the Puerto Ricans is more complicated. Only the case of the much smaller Portuguese group, among whom were the colored Bravas, offers an analogy among other American immigrants. A sharp sense of color difference was not characteristic of the island, which recognized the formal equality of all, despite some discrimination against the darker-skinned individuals who were associated with lower-class status. In Puerto Rico, light mulattoes were accepted as whites. Yet the presence of the Negroes in New York and consciousness of the national problem have created a high degree of awareness of the importance of color.[41]

By island definitions, some 75 per cent of the population of Puerto Rico were white, some 25 per cent were colored. Whatever data we have indicates that a larger percentage of white than of colored Puerto Ricans came to the mainland. There they found themselves in a dilemma, for color which was of slight importance back home was crucial in New York. The effect has been to strengthen the character of the identification of the Puerto Rican in the case of those who were colored and to weaken it in the case of those who were white. The colored Puerto Rican wished above all to avoid the stigma of identification with the Negro and he could do so only by establishing himself as a Spanish-speaking Puerto Rican. On the other hand, whiteness became an important asset to the remainder of the Puerto Ricans in this country. As soon as some improvement of status enabled them to escape, there was an incentive to dissolve the ties with the group and to lose themselves in the general category of whites. This was particularly important in the second and third generations, as the difficulty of securing any reliable estimate of the number testifies.

Two alternative directions of development are open for the future. Which will be followed will depend not only upon the Puerto Ricans themselves but also upon the general estimate of color in the whole community. If color consciousness grows more intense and the penalties of identification by color grow more severe, the Puerto Rican group may be fragmented into three parts. The continuing flow of new arrivals will struggle to maintain themselves as Puerto Ricans. The colored Puerto Ricans already settled, and particularly those of the second and third generations for whom the difference of language fades in importance, will be pressed toward an identification with the more numerous Negroes. And the white majority of second and third generation Puerto Ricans who lose the consciousness of language will find an ever-growing incentive to drop their identification and to merge with some other surrounding ethnic community.

The alternative premises a decline in the consciousness of color. In that case the white and colored Puerto Ricans in the awareness of their common identity could develop a coherent community to which newcomers would be added and which would grow stronger through immigration. Its identity would thus be preserved over a much longer period.

Which of these alternatives is followed will depend in some part on the reactions of the larger community. As far as the Puerto Ricans are concerned, there seems to be a growing consciousness of, and pride in, their group identity. That may reflect their preference for the second alternative, if the penalties of following it do not become too great.

The answers to these questions are thus related to the structure of communal life that Negroes and Puerto Ricans have developed in the city. But before those can be meaningfully considered it will be necessary to examine in greater detail their patterns of adjustment to metropolitan living. The difficulties they have thus far encountered and the degree to which they have surmounted them will throw some light on their history during the past half-century and on their prospects for the future.

4

Patterns of Adjustment

Too often a sense of panic at the presence of strangers has obscured the understanding of the process by which they become parts of the community to which they migrate. This is as true of the Negroes and Puerto Ricans as it was of their predecessors. That panic leads to exaggerated estimates of the numbers involved, as when responsible newspapers guessed that there were 600,000 Puerto Ricans in the city at a time when it held a little more than one-fourth that number.[1]

The same kind of fear also created an exaggerated impression of the novelty of contemporary urban problems. Too often it was assumed that there was precedent neither for the diffusion of New York's population into its suburbs, nor for the reception in the city of groups like the Negroes and the Puerto Ricans.[2]

The data for historical comparison indicates that, in adjusting to metropolitan life, the Negroes and the Puerto Ricans faced problems similar to those already encountered by earlier immigrants. The transition from rural to urban surroundings was difficult in itself, and it was complicated by serious cultural discrepancies between the old life and the new. Like their predecessors also, the Negroes and Puerto Ricans filled the lowest occupations and suffered in consequence from poverty, inferior housing, and their concomitant social disorders.

There were, however, two significant differences between these and earlier immigrants. The Negroes and Puerto Ricans found their adjustment complicated by their dark skins in a period when a great deal of social tension focused on the issue of color difference. Furthermore, there had been significant changes in the character of the metropolitan community to which they came. In 1820, the scale of settlement was small enough so that neighborhood, city, and region were identical. In 1850 region and city were still the same, but the districts of residence had been differentiated in a variety of neighborhoods. Twenty years later the urban region had spread beyond the city's political boundaries. In 1900 the municipality had expanded to take in that part of the region within New York State. Since then still more rapid diffusion of the population has broadened the region, reduced the relative size of the city, and altered the character of the neighborhood. Those changes in the context of metropolitan life are certainly factors in establishing the pattern of adjustment by Negroes and Puerto Ricans.

It will be well to begin the analysis of that pattern with an examination of the total social context within which it developed. A consideration of certain broad changes in the whole New York community and of the experience of the older ethnic groups in the region since 1928 will supply a background against which the problems of the Negroes and the Puerto Ricans can be more meaningfully evaluated.

New York in the 1920's seemed to be entering upon a period of stability. With the end of large-scale immigration from Europe and the slackening of the rate of population growth, there was often talk in that decade that the city had reached an era of maturity. It seemed to be approaching a turning point beyond which it would cease to expand and be compelled to plan within limited resources. The very concern with regional planning in these years reflected that conviction. This sentiment was fortified by the onset of the depression, a time for retrenchment and for a careful hoarding of resources. This atmosphere suffused the years down to the outbreak of the war in 1941.

There followed a period, which has lasted until the present, of renewed expansion and of prosperity. The new conditions were significantly reflected in changes in both social and economic trends. The revival of business activity and of relatively full employment, the reappearance of labor shortages, and the rise in family incomes transformed the basic material terms of life in the city. These conditions were associated with the growing stability of family life, the rise in the birth rate, and the resumption of population growth.

The result of both trends was a renewal of the process of rapid expansion to the suburbs which had slackened noticeably in the 1930's. The move out of the central city was associated, as it had been in the past, with the difficulties of accommodating middle-class ideals to the practical problems of urban life. The renewed emphasis on the togetherness of a sound family relationship and the desirability of rearing children in good neighborhoods led directly back to the one-family house on its own plot. The virtues of home ownership and of the high status that it brought now, however, could only be attained outside the city limits; population growth and rising land values made that certain, and inexorably stimulated the shift to the suburbs.

The postwar dispersal of residences bore striking similarities to earlier movements of population from the city. But the patterns of commuting that developed with it were distinctive in several important respects. The fact that a good deal of industry was now located on the outskirts meant that a good deal of passenger traffic moved to work around the periphery and from the city outward as well as toward the center. More important, this movement, unlike those of the past, was not accompanied by an extension of public transportation. The automobile made it possible for many individuals and groups to move about freely and to select their residences almost without reference to their place of work. But it also led to significant contractions of the services available through public transportation; and high costs made additions to those facilities impossible.

This factor magnified the differential among income groups. In the absence of public transportation it became more difficult for the less well-to-do to follow the more prosperous to the suburbs. The man without an automobile of his own had access only to a contracting area of settlement. That in turn intensified the association between suburban residence and status.

The alternation of depression and prosperity, of contraction and expansion, helped to explain the development of the older ethnic groups in the city. In the decade or so after 1928, a general sense of tightness led to widespread fear of the loss of position. Those who were already well established were on the defensive, while groups which were seeking to become established felt greater pressure than ever before. The situation heightened the consciousness of group identity; it placed a high premium on belonging to the proper groups and attached a strong handicap to belonging to the improper ones. An uneasy suspicion that the opportunities of the future might be more restricted than those of the past made discrimination in employment and in education more intense than ever before. At every level there was a marked desire to hold on—the Anglo-Saxons to their professional and managerial positions, the Irish and Germans to their places as clerks or skilled craftsmen.

There remained some measure of social mobility. The sons of unskilled workers were still becoming lawyers or teachers or being trained for those positions, particularly among the newer groups like the Italians and the Jews. This was due in part to the continued vitality of the conception of equality of opportunity in most sectors of the educational system; in part it was due to a change in the character of the labor force, within which many fewer unskilled hands were needed. But for the moment this occupational upgrading had unfortunate consequences. It meant that more people were prepared for the better places in the economy than could be absorbed under current economic conditions. The result was a high degree of tension between the groups moving up and those already established, with the latter using various devices of discrimination to their own advantage.

The tension of the struggle for status was reflected most acutely in the competition for desirable housing. The Jews and the Italians pressed on into better neighborhoods, moving steadily out of Manhattan into Brooklyn and the Bronx as the spread of apartment houses made facilities available to them. As earlier, the process displaced the older residents. But now such shifts evoked bitterness and resentment often exacerbated through the influence of real estate brokers who feared that patterns of open occupancy would have an unsettling effect upon values. Falling prices for housing entailed substantial costs for people who had to sell. As the "tip-point" approached in a neighborhood and it became clear that its character would change, fear of financial losses added to the general sense of insecurity among established groups. Informal methods of restriction through restrictive covenants or gentlemen's agreements became the last desperate line of defense against social as well as pecuniary loss.[3]

Such threats to the external symbols of status were at the root of the group conflicts of the late 1930's. The activities of the Christian Front, of the *Brooklyn Tablet,* and of similar movements had a particular attraction to the threatened Irish and Germans for they stood in greatest danger from the adverse effects of the depression. But the strain was felt also by the Jews and Italians who considered themselves under attack and blocked off from the opportunities for advancement. For people who were established, ethnic identification was a badge of their status, while for those who were seeking to become established it was a token of that which held them back.

The change since 1939 and particularly since 1945 has been striking. Every index shows a noteworthy decline in discrimination in employment. Slight pockets of prejudice against Jews and Italians persist only in a limited number of jobs, such as those of hotel desk clerks, in which a stereotyped appearance remains important; and these are rarely worth competing for. More generally, favorable economic conditions, the disrepute into which discrimination fell during the war, and the fair employment practices act have gone a long way toward resolving this problem.

With the renewal of prosperity and the disappearance of unemployment, the competition for jobs gave way to a competition for men. The transformation of the labor force through which the number of professional, managerial, and clerical places grew while the number of unskilled jobs declined, now made itself felt more positively.[4] Shortages were particularly prominent in those areas which had seemed most restricted before 1939—in the professions and the ranks of skilled labor. In ironic contrast with the situation before the war, some medical schools were undersubscribed and the heavy demands for doctors, teachers, and engineers could not be filled. These shortages, combined with a more intense transformation of the labor force, eased the problem of social mobility. Wide areas toward the top of the occupational ladder were now thrown open for the advance of the children of the laborers. Middle-class status was therefore within the reach of many second and third generation new immigrant families. As discrimination declined and opportunities widened, ethnic identification ceased to be a serious impediment.

This change coincided with a rise in the birth rate and a strengthening of family life, both of which were now also associated with middle-class status. The result was a renewed trend toward movement out of apartments and into single-family houses, away from the center of the city and into the suburbs. The trend was stimulated by government policy which eased the process of acquiring small homes and also by the great emphasis on education which was connected with the future advancement of children.

The result was a concerted shift toward the periphery by all those who aspired to a rise in status. Between 1950 and 1957 an outburst of new construction, wherever in the region empty land was available, put numerous new dwelling units at the disposal of those who sought improved housing and contributed to the massive movement of population outside the central city. Only those too fixed in their ways to break familiar neighborhood ties or too old to hope for a change in career remained in the earlier centers of settlement; and such people required relatively little space. Clusters of Italians thus stayed in Greenwich Village and of Jews in the East Side. A few young married couples moved into new apartment projects, drawn before their babies arrived by the attractiveness of urban life. But they hardly compensated for those who left. The East Side and Manhattan in general lost steadily in number of residents; and there was a general decline in the density of settlement of the most heavily populated areas of the city.[5]

The automobile and new highway systems had thrown open an

immense region of suburban residences into which the growing population moved. The areas of desirable homes were more sharply detached from the areas of production and, to a significant degree, remoteness from the center of the city became a measure of income.

The movement was still one by groups, for the values of the suburb could best be realized within an ethnic mold. It would be fruitless to attempt to map the specific migration of each of the many groups that participated in the process; but the general characteristics of the migration are clear. The new suburbs recreated in a modified form the patterns of life of the old neighborhoods. Yet the rapid widening of the total area of settlement removed the sharpness of competition among ethnic groups; so much space became available that one did not have to interfere with another. While a few very select neighborhoods are still closed by gentlemen's agreements and restrictive covenants, even these devices are surreptitious and on the way toward disappearance.[6]

Two factors in particular eased competition. Since the value of real estate was rising, people who left a neighborhood generally profited when they sold their homes. Furthermore, the very motives that induced the move to the suburbs heightened the consciousness of ethnic identity. Family feeling, the desire to preserve connections with children, the need for communal ways of expending leisure time, and the search for social identity emphasized the value of belonging to churches, societies, and similar ethnic organizations.

These associations showed a striking vitality. Although their ranks were no longer being replenished by immigration, they gained strength through the acquisition of an indigenous quality that relieved them of the taint of foreignness. After 1945, the religious element was more often stressed in these affiliations than earlier; but within the broadly recognized categories of Protestant, Catholic, and Jew, narrower groups retained their individuality as did some outside those categories, like the Greeks and Russians. Even when these associations lost their original function, as when the government after 1933 assumed many of the burdens formerly carried by private philanthropic or benefit societies, they shifted to some other basis.

What was critical was the sense of identification they gave their members, not the specific task they performed. And which identification was much less important than the desire for some identification. Belonging to some group was more and more often what mattered, not belonging to any particular one. Often an individual now found it difficult to attain the kind of anonymity that the city provided in the 1920's; but he was no longer penalized for the affiliations toward which ethnic ties drew him.

Since being an Italian or a Jew no longer bore the odium of distinctive inferiority, ethnic preferences entered prominently into the choice of residence, often outweighing such other considerations as access to the place of employment. The result was a decline in the competition for common space and, therefore, a reduction of tension. The last twenty years have thus presented a marked contrast to the ten that preceded them.

Movement to the suburbs was thus an indication of the establishment of a new relation among place of residence, occupational status, family stability, and the ethnic community, a relation established in the context of postwar economic expansion. That relation, not the simple facts of the spread of settlement or the character of the Negroes and Puerto Ricans, is at the heart of the problems of adjustment of the present and of the immediate future.

The changes in the character of the wider community have shaped the course of Negro and Puerto Rican adjustment in the past three decades. From 1929 to the end of the 1930's both groups suffered from the precarious effects of the depression. From 1939 onward, the shortage of unskilled labor relieved them of the economic burdens of marginal employment but compelled them to confront the new problems of group life.

Both groups entered the labor market, as earlier immigrants did, at the bottom of the occupational hierarchy. Neither in the South nor in Puerto Rico had these immigrants been able to accumulate education or capital. Furthermore, the Negroes were hampered by color and the Puerto Ricans by ignorance of English. But more important was the fact that, as newcomers, they had to accept whatever jobs were available. Even those who arrived with skills or had had training in white collar occupations had to take whatever places were offered to them.

As a result they became mostly unskilled marginal laborers. The earliest forms of employment they found were in the construction and garment industries which had formerly depended on Europeans. The earlier gains of New York's Negroes were now wiped out by the inundation from the South. The black men, like the Puerto Ricans, were frequently unemployed; their wages were low; and their conditions of labor were poor. They had therefore to supplement their incomes through the labor of women, in homework, shops, or domestic service. Both groups had come to accept such additional earnings at home.[7]

The depression struck the Negroes with particular severity. Since they were in an exposed position by virtue of their marginal status in the labor force, they were the first to be fired and the last to be rehired. And since they had few resources they were vulnerable to every setback. The decade of the 1930's therefore was one of unremitting hardship. The gap between the median family incomes of the Negroes and Puetro Ricans on the one hand and of non-Puerto Rican whites on the other widened; and a careful student at the end of the decade could see little prospect of improvement.[8]

The renewed demand for manpower after 1939 eased the employment problem; and prosperity enabled the growing number of Negroes and Puerto Ricans to find remunerative places, despite those aspects of the occupational pattern that tended to diminish the dependence of the economy on unskilled labor and despite the shrinkage in number of jobs relative to industrial output. Although the continued inflow of newcomers who were unskilled or who faced a period of adjustment to the new situation added to the number of low-paid laborers in the city, these were not as helpless as their predecessors. They came with superior information on job prospects and could return if disappointed. They did not therefore constitute the massive pool of hands with no alternative at all that had been available to the region's low-wage industries in the 1850's or 1890's or even the 1930's.

Family incomes rose steadily after 1940 and the differential between Negroes and Puerto Ricans on the one hand and non-Puerto Rican whites on the other narrowed perceptibly. The disparity in earnings in the 1950's was less likely to spring from differences in the rate of pay for a given job than from the fact that the Negroes and Puerto Ricans were clustered in the least rewarding occupations. The improvement in the economic situation of these groups was the product of prosperity, of trade union activity, and of conscious government policy embodied in the state fair employment practices act.[9]

The effective reduction of unemployment and the elimination of discriminatory wage scales only clarified another and more fundamental problem—that of how the members of these groups were to be enabled to repeat the climb out of the ranks of unskilled labor to which ever more of them aspired. The general insecurity of these people and their recency in the city emphasized the importance of internal distinctions and put a substantial premium on the ability to rise in occupational status. The inclination of their press to identify every individual in terms of his salary illustrated the weight ascribed by Negroes and Puerto Ricans to the level of earnings.

Thus far they have had only limited and qualified success in escaping from unskilled labor. At the start two traditional avenues of upward mobility were open to the Negroes and Puerto Ricans as they had been to earlier immigrants—the first in areas in which they dealt with members of their own groups, the second in areas in which talent had the opportunity to assert itself without suffering from the limitations of their ethnic backgrounds.

The first Negro opportunities came through enterprises which catered to colored people and which depended upon the patronage of their neighbors. Madame C. J. Walker, who early in the century had earned a fortune through the sale of a hair straightener, was a classic example. Barber and beauty shops, funeral parlors, restaurants, bars, liquor stores, night clubs, and other small businesses are sprinkled through the Negro districts—about 5,000 of them in Harlem, 2,000 elsewhere in the city. The expansion of the total size of the group has gradually increased the potential support for establishments of this sort. The Puerto Ricans similarly moved out of the ranks of labor by opening groceries, meat markets, *bodegas,* and other little shops that catered to the distinctive tastes of their fellows.[10]

The patronage of both groups also maintained a certain number of professional men, lawyers, insurance and real estate brokers, and doctors, who added to the middle-class element in the population. Somewhat incongruously, entry to that status was also possible for a limited number who earned their wealth through policy and other forms of gambling and through rackets associated with narcotics, vice, unions, and business. These callings, which existed on, and over, the margin of legality, had always offered opportunities to outsiders not as inhibited as established respectable Americans in their attitudes toward alcohol, sex, lotteries, or violence. They now afforded some Negroes and Puerto Ricans a means of rising.[11]

The second channel of mobility was much narrower and opened an escape from labor to a still smaller group. But it had a high symbolic value, since through it were available both wealth and recognition by the whites. In the theater, art, music, and athletic worlds, talent was more or less absolute; and discrimination was much less effective than in other realms. This accounted for the high incentive among Negroes and Puerto Ricans to seek these pursuits as a way up; and it accounted also for the popularity and high status among them of prize fighters, musicians, and the like, a popularity of which the incidence of reference in magazines and newspapers is a striking index.[12]

All these means of rising are, however, self-contained and limited. They are more available to some elements of the Negro and Puerto Rican population than to others; the West Indian colored people, for instance, are better prepared for urban life and more aggressive than the natives, and have profited as a result. But, in sum total, such economic opportunities affect only very small numbers. Furthermore, they depend upon the maintenance of group solidarity; and, to the extent that these immigrants become adjusted to the New York environment, such means of rising may actually become less effective and still more limited. Paradoxically, the decline in discrimination has already had that effect. In recent years the Negroes have been relatively well treated in mid-town and Bronx stores; they have been accorded charge facilities and improved services. Chain and department stores also earn good will by advertising in the ethnic media. As a result a substantial part of expenditures has been diverted away from local shops. Buying downtown, in fact, is sometimes a sign of superior status. Such trends certainly have weakened the position of the retailer or professional who depends upon an ethnic clientele.[13]

Some sectors of both the Negro and Puerto Rican population accept the situation and grow bitter or apathetic in consequence— with deleterious social effects. But a substantial and growing percentage, particularly in the second generation, are determined to find wider and better ways out. Only a few succeed as well as the Negro doctor in Sheepshead Bay, four-fifths of whose patients are white. But the number who seek the widest scope for their abilities is constantly expanding; and the second generation shows a perceptible rise in occupational level over the first.[14]

To some extent some such people have managed to escape from unskilled labor by moving into the service trades, occupations that are better paid than jobs in industry and yet in which they do not compete at a disadvantage against better established elements of the labor force. Here too there are significant limits however; and the fact that the Puerto Ricans have done better than the Negroes in these fields reflects the continuing importance of color prejudice as a selective factor.

Beyond this level, moreover, the hardships of achieving a rise in status are magnified. It is difficult to measure the extent to which such a rise has already taken place. But it is possible to analyze the factors that condition the capacity of these groups to move upward.

Their predecessors climbed either as entrepreneurs or as fee- or salary-receiving skilled employees. In both respects the Negroes and

Puerto Ricans, for the moment, stand at a disadvantage as compared with earlier immigrants.

The failure is not due primarily to ethnic attributes. There has been some disposition to blame the lag in Negro development on their lack of capacity for business; the failure of the caterers to expand early in the century, for instance, has often been ascribed to their inability, as a group, to adopt modern methods or to adjust to new conditions. Or, alternatively, their slowness as compared with the Puerto Ricans or Chinese has been ascribed to cultural traits, ethnically determined.[15]

There is some validity to these explanations. But it is essential, in advancing them, to treat them in the context both of the conditions created by color prejudice and of the economic terms within which business now operates.

The cultural traits which handicap the Negro entrepreneur are closely related to the prejudice from which he has suffered. Thus, it seems true that the Negroes find it particularly difficult to develop the practices of saving, or to hold on to a surplus that can be used as capital, or to transmit to their children the nest egg that will permit them to make an advantageous start in life. This difficulty is, in part, a result of the peculiar patterns of consumer expenditure within the group. Like other people whose income has been uncertain and sporadic they have wasteful spending habits. The recollection of long periods of deprivation encourages "mad spending sprees" when funds become available. There is a kind of pride in reading that a housekeeper who inherits $10,000 buys a big car; that a stewardess has a $1,000 perfume collection; that a windfall is splurged on a wardrobe; or that a picnic at the Kerhonson Country Club consumes 1,000 chickens and 200 fifths of whiskey. In addition, the heavy cost of funerals, the temptation of debt with its heavy concealed charges, and inexperience in the techniques of economical urban shopping needlessly eat up family resources.[16] Yet, beyond these particular manifestations of inadequate management lies a more general sense of insecurity and uncertainty about the future that weakens incentives for saving. In the absence of clearly defined, attainable objects, in the absence sometimes even of the hope for improvement, it seems futile to economize and no loss to seek the pleasures of the moment in immediate consumption. Significantly, the Negroes who most frequently have capital available for investment are ministers and other salaried and professional men whose incomes run above the levels of expenditure accepted as appropriate for them. In that respect the Negroes seem closer to the Irish of the past than to the Jews or Italians.

The difference in the experience of the Puerto Ricans is enlightening. To some, but to a lesser, extent, the Puerto Rican immigrants bring with them habits that also discourage capital accumulation. They come from the class least likely to save at home; and even those who did hold on to surpluses were accustomed to investing it only in real estate. They too were likely to contract a high volume of debt and to show few liquid assets. Yet, from among these newcomers, as from among the West Indian Negroes, a substantially larger percentage of entrepreneurs have emerged. In part that was due to the fact that on the island the shopkeeper was a familiar figure and even the jíbaro was acquainted with the idea that through trade one could achieve a rise in status. But it was also due to the fact that color has not been for the Puerto Ricans as determining a barrier as for the Negro; and they have in the very act of migration often defined their own goals of improvement.[17]

However, the advantage is relative only. For all these groups, external factors, derived from the changing context within which business operates, are even more of an impediment than ethnic traits. The Puerto Ricans do not suffer from the same handicaps as the Negroes and yet face almost as much difficulty in establishing themselves. The path of the independent small businessman who aims to break out from within the limited patronage of the ethnic circle is more difficult now than earlier. There are still vestiges of the tradition by which the peddler became a shopkeeper and then a department store owner; or by which the grocer became a wholesaler or distributor; or by which the subcontractor became a manufacturer. But it is not as easy now as formerly to move along these lines. For everyone, the growing advantages of bigness put the small and new competitor at a disadvantage. Suburban shopping centers remote from the center of town make expansion difficult for entrepreneurs who begin with the limited patronage of a neighborhood ethnic group. As a result it seems unlikely that independent small business will provide an important access to a future rise in status for either group.

The fact that the capital required is larger and more difficult to come by is particularly burdensome to these groups. On the one hand, their own members are not given to corporate investment, especially since the Negroes at least still have bitter recollections of the disastrous outcome of Marcus Garvey's enterprises in the 1920's. The only financial institution run by colored people is the Carver Savings and Loan Association. On the other hand, both groups find it difficult to negotiate business loans, not only because of overt prejudice but even more because of persistent stereotypes among bankers of what constitutes a good risk.[18]

The alternative to entrepreneurship as a means of rising is to break into the developing complex of positions as professional, managerial, or clerical employees and fee receivers. This channel of advancement is likely in the future to be much more important than in the past. Economic and social trends, which have magnified the importance of large enterprise and of government, have also expanded the clerical, managerial, and professional ranks in the American economy, so that these now seem the most accessible means of rising. Yet, although access to these situations depends less upon inherited wealth or connections than upon skill, prejudice and certain stereotypes of suitability have heretofore restricted the number of eligible Negroes and Puerto Ricans in them. Resentment at exclusion from such positions led to organized protests by the Citizens League for Fair Play, as far back as 1933. But the general restriction of opportunities in that decade kept such protests ineffective.

The importance of discrimination in this area has become clear since the end of the depression. The difficulty of Negroes and Puerto Ricans in penetrating it, despite the vast expansion of opportunities, stands in contrast to the experience of other prewar minorities like the Jews and Italians, who have had the advantage of a longer residence in the city and who also have not been burdened by the handicap of color.[19]

There are signs of improvement although the pace is slow. Substantial numbers of Puerto Ricans and Negroes show an avid desire for advancement that is reflected in a widespread interest in commercial education. As in the case of the Irish earlier, the first breakthrough has been in government employment. Apart from the greater sensitivity of the state as an employer to the issue of public policy involved in discrimination, the growing weight of the Negro and Puerto Rican groups as a political factor has produced openings in the civil service. There has been a steady penetration of the police and fire departments, the public schools, and the offices of municipal, state, and federal agencies.[20]

Politics also became the means for wider social action. The state fair employment practices act forbade discrimination on the grounds of race or ethnic origin. It had an effect upon certain labor unions and large-scale employers and set a standard of practices that was important, whatever the degree of enforcement. The machinery of administration in the State Commission Against Discrimination is relatively weak but the effects of the standard it sets are significant. The rise in importance of the Negroes and Puerto Ricans as consumers has similarly influenced employers anxious to have their patronage. Finally, the growing concern of the trade unions in the metropolitan area with the problem has operated in the same direction.[21]

The effects of the more general drop in bias are not readily measurable. A recent study by the State Commission on Discrimination of the hotel industry in New York City showed a striking penetration into some of these jobs but within significantly restricted limits. In the first place the Puerto Ricans have made more progress than the Negroes; and the advance for either group has been slightest in the case of white-collared administrative positions in which the employee comes in contact with the public, that is, in which appearance is important. Both restrictions indicate that color remains a barrier to such employment.[22]

While prejudice and discrimination are real and important factors they do not in themselves complete the picture. For, while they operate to depress the condition of the Negroes and Puerto Ricans, they are reinforced by deficiencies in the education and preparation of many individuals in those groups. Ironically, for instance, after the airlines had been persuaded in 1958 to hire colored hostesses, it proved difficult to find an appropriate applicant. Altogether apart from the factor of prejudice, the number of qualified applicants is not as large as it was in the case of earlier groups at a comparable stage of development. Discrimination has thus depressed the underprivileged while the conditions produced by deprivation become the grounds—or at least the pretext—for continued discrimination.[23]

The connection between the schools and social mobility makes the educational system of special concern to the Negroes and Puerto Ricans. For, through the schools the lower elements of the labor force, or at least their children, have in the past and may in the future acquire the means of pulling themselves upward economically. In both groups conscientious parents continue to believe in that possibility.[24]

Hence the great concern of both groups with the school system, even beyond its vocational and trade aspects. There are efforts to encourage participation in the P.T.A.'s; and the press regularly notes evidence of scholastic honors or achievements and publicizes the availability of scholarships. But the Negroes and Puerto Ricans nevertheless feel that they are deprived of genuine equality of educational opportunity. The problem arises in part from the fact that so many of these people are immigrants and in part from the conditions they encounter on arrival.[25]

In 1910, before the migration northward became serious, the level of literacy of the Blacks was only slightly below that of the whites in the city.[26] But in the next four decades the relation changed as the newcomers paid the price for retardation in the areas from which they came. There has been more recent improvement both in the South and in Puerto Rico. But some gap remains and is reflected in the fact that the median number of school years for both groups is lower than that for whites. There is also evidence of an unusually high level of absenteeism among children within the legal school age.[27]

To some extent the deficiency in preparation is reinforced by the conditions children from these groups find upon arrival. A variety of factors prevent many of them from concentrating upon their studies—the inability to use correct English, their own poverty and sometimes the necessity for part-time work, the lack of privacy at home, and the remoteness of the goals toward which education leads. The result is often a high rate of truancy. All too often, also, even those students who attend docilely merely sit out their lessons, without the incentive to pay attention to what transpires in the classroom.[28]

The parents are sometimes inclined to ascribe all these difficulties to discrimination against them by the educational system. There is some, but not total, validity to these complaints. Public schools in New York City and in the other communities of the metropolitan area are not segregated by law; assignments are made primarily on the basis of residence. But in homogeneous neighborhoods in which most children have a common ethnic background, the schools are in effect segregated without legal formality and reflect the character of the population in their district. The process is cumulative. Members of other groups caught within the boundaries of a Negro or Puerto Rican district flee to the suburbs or to the private schools. That offers the individual a refuge, but often only compounds the general difficulty, for the result has been a perceptible change in the character of the public schools. The report of the Superintendent of Schools for 1957 showed a drop of 20,000 in the number of white pupils, 12,740 of them having left for Long Island, 4,781 for New Jersey, and 2,606 for Westchester and Rockland counties. Negroes then formed 20.1 per cent and Puerto Ricans 15.4 per cent of the school population. But they were highly concentrated. Fully 455 of the 704 schools in the city were homogeneous to the extent that 90 per cent or more of their students were either Negro or white or Puerto Rican.[29]

Given the nature of the neighborhoods in which they live, it is not surprising that the education of Negro and Puerto Rican children should proceed generally under inferior conditions. The schools they attend are, by their very character, housed in the oldest buildings, have the least desirable reputations, and are shunned by the best teachers.

There has been some conscious effort to meet the special needs of these groups, and particularly the language problems of the Puerto Ricans. But the difficulties created by residential segregation are not readily surmountable. Many Negro parents, alive to the importance of the problem, are sensitive or suspicious of any arrangement that hints at discrimination; and there has been some pressure on the Board of Education to effect a change by altering the lines of the school districts and the procedures for teacher assignment. This is unlikely to give more than minor relief, however. To prove really effective such changes would call for a total readjustment of the city's educational pattern; and the losses entailed in doing so might well nullify any social gains.[30]

The experience of earlier groups shows the importance of three other modes of coping with the problem of providing equal educational opportunities throughout the society. There ought, of course, to be a general improvement of all schools. More important, a decline in discrimination that would ease the prospects of upward mobility and put the rewards of education within reach of the minorities would give such pupils the incentive that would itself raise the level of their schooling. It would also give more scope for the recognition of individual differences among students. The lack of such incentives has been as great an educational deterrent for children of these groups in New York as it was in the South or in Puerto Rico. Finally, greater freedom of movement would extend to the Negroes and Puerto Ricans, or to selective groups among them, the opportunity to escape to better neighborhoods and better schools.[31]

Education is thus linked not only with the problems of occupational mobility but also with those of housing, which is likely to prove the most critical area of social conflict in the next two decades.

The Negroes and Puerto Ricans in the Region at first followed patterns of settlement similar to those of the earlier immigrant groups. In the last two decades of the nineteenth century, the Negroes were rather dispersed throughout the city. There were two substantial clusters: one in lower Manhattan around Sullivan and Bleecker Streets and Minetta Lane; and another in the west side tract bounded by 26th and 31st Streets and by Sixth and Eighth Avenues. They were soon pushed out of both areas of concentration, however. After 1890, the poorer Italians pushed them out of one; and the changes that followed upon the construction of the Pennsylvania Station forced them out of the other. In 1910 they were therefore still highly scattered, with the highest concentrations in the Thirteenth and Twenty-first Assembly Districts. Almost 60 per cent of them lived outside the six Assembly Districts in which they formed more than 5 per cent of the population.[32]

Downtown the spread of Italian settlement into Greenwich Village prevented the establishment of a solid colored neighborhood. But the Negroes had meanwhile acquired a foothold east of Lenox Avenue in Harlem where overbuilding had made space available to them. Housing here was, at the start, tolerable, although the practice of taking in lodgers became common, as it was among immigrants. But the situation deteriorated rapidly after 1915 when the swift expansion in the number of colored people strained available accommodations. Significantly, the newly arriving southern Negroes settled not on the East Side where the population was declining faster than the housing inventory, but in Harlem to which they were drawn by the initial superiority of the available quarters and by the existence of a neighborhood with which they could identify themselves. Successive districts in Harlem were soon vacated by the departure of many of the Jews and Italians who moved away to the Bronx. The percentage of Negroes who owned their homes dropped;

and a densely settled community grew rapidly in the 1920's. Harlem then developed the familiar features of slum life.[33]

The strain grew more intense in the next decade. The complication of color prejudice which limited the freedom of the individual to select his own place of residence and of the depression which lowered the earning power of the whole group meant that its ability to move out of this district was even narrower than it had been for earlier newcomers. The very wealthiest could buy homes out of town; and small clusters of high-cost colored housing appeared, as on 139th Street between Seventh and Eighth Avenues and on "Sugar Hill" (Edgecombe between St. Nicholas and Convent Avenues). But, more generally, it was difficult even for those who were rising to break away since they were so markedly identified. The vast majority whose economic conditions remained depressed found it impossible to move or to keep their standards of housing from deteriorating.[34]

Furthermore, the prolonged fall in real estate values during the depression made any shift in population more difficult and embittered those who felt the pressure of Negro competition. When the colored people outgrew the limitations of Harlem, they found few neighborhoods into which they could move. Hemmed in in Manhattan, some of them poured over into the Bedford-Stuyvesant section of Brooklyn, where a small group had settled earlier. That area quickly took on the character of another Harlem. Since rents rose when Negroes moved in, space was at a premium. Perhaps a quarter of the Negroes in these districts could find no better accommodations than as lodgers, sometimes even being compelled to share "hot beds," although rent then consumed fully 40 per cent of the income of half the colored families.[35]

The influence of public housing in the 1930's was generally in the direction of stabilizing the status quo and preserving the Negroes' segregation. The F.H.A. and the H.O.L.C. adopted the principle of the realtors' codes against sales or rentals to "inharmonious racial groups"; and that simply froze the colored people where they were.

Nor was any governmental agency then concerned with breaking down the barriers against the spread of the Negroes; none of the planning of this period took any regard of the human elements that might be involved. In the absence of any attention to ethnic considerations, existing patterns of segregation were only extended and intensified.[36]

There was no relief from the immediate effects of the war. The end of unemployment raised family incomes and solved some of the most critical economic problems of the group. But the Negroes were now immobilized by the acute housing shortage; and the frustrations of those years were clearly involved in the violence of the race riot of 1943.[37]

Since the end of the war there has been some relaxation of tension, but no solution to the housing problem. Less than 1 per cent of the city's housing resources were vacant in 1950 so that newcomers had to compete with established residents for space. And, while the total housing inventory of the region grew more rapidly than the population in the next seven years, it was built at such high cost that only 5 per cent of new construction was taken up by nonwhites. Meanwhile Negroes had occupied one-half the units in structures demolished in the same period. Color, low incomes, and the accumulated lag in remedying the housing shortage have thus complicated the problems of the Negro as they had not those of other groups.[38]

The bulk of the nonwhite population remains in the two prewar colored districts. Most of Manhattan's 300,000 Negroes are still in Harlem, with smaller pockets on the lower East Side and the middle West Side; and Bedford-Stuyvesant contains the bulk of those in Brooklyn. In addition, two new areas of Negro penetration have been opened up in Morrisania (the Bronx) and South Jamaica-St. Albans (Queens) by the move to the outer suburbs of the older residents. Maps of changes in Negro settlement between 1930 and 1950 show that expansion has been largely into contiguous blocks and that the degree of dispersion has often actually declined since the war.[39]

The older Negro districts are still slums, despite the efforts at clearance since 1945. That they are somewhat better than Negro slums in other cities hardly makes them more acceptable to their residents. Occasional elegant apartment houses and public housing projects do little to mitigate the misery of the masses. Three times as many nonwhites as whites occupy substandard dwellings in the city. The Negroes are far less likely to own their own dwellings, they are more crowded, they occupy older buildings, and they have gained less since 1940 than the whites. Part of that difference is economic; the gap between Black and white narrows as one descends the social scale. But it exists everywhere and has its source in the prejudice that deprives the Negro of the free choice of his residence.[40]

Some of the outlying communities in the region have passed through a comparable development. The number of Negroes in such municipalities as Mt. Vernon and New Rochelle in Westchester County and Newark, East Orange, Jersey City, and Montclair in New Jersey has been growing rapidly. The nonwhite population of Newark alone has risen to some 130,000 or one-fourth of that city's total.

The expansion of Negro settlement in these areas created problems similar to those in Manhattan. Already in 1910, for instance, Newark and Jersey City had their own little Harlems; 43 per cent of the colored population of those towns lived in the wards with high Negro concentrations. The tendency toward clustering persisted with the growth in the number of Negroes since 1910. Indeed the difficulties in the way of dispersal may actually be less imposing in the five boroughs than in New Jersey, Westchester, and Long Island where the suburban tradition of the Negro as a servant and inferior has in the past been more prominent than urban cosmopolitanism.[41]

The quest for adequate housing is a serious problem for all Negroes in the Metropolitan Region. But the configuration of the problem differs decidedly with the level of family income. In discerning the patterns of movement that may have significance for the future it is necessary to hold those distinctions clearly in mind.

The shift of a low-income colored family to a new location within the region is not always a voluntary move and is influenced but slightly by such considerations as proximity to the place of employment or the kind of education available to children. Such people, when they are not simply shifting aimlessly about from flat to flat, generally move as a result of external pressure rather than out of the confident expectation of improving their residences. Often they are relocated as a result of the clearance of the old housing they occupied. They are not averse to a change of address. But they are concerned, with justification, with being placed in less desirable circumstances than before. Even if the new location is not physically inferior to the old, they are reluctant to break neighborhood ties of long standing.

The most desirable dislocation which can occur to the low-income family is the movement to a public housing project within the city or within the other municipalities which have dealt with the problem. More than 90,000 families have thus been accommodated in New York City alone, 38 per cent of them Negro. The figures of the New York City Housing Authority show a sizable percentage increase in the colored population of the various public housing units, particularly of those which require an annual income of less than $6,000 for eligibility. Most of these people formerly lived on the site cleared for the project or they were residents of substandard units in other areas of the city and qualified according to the standards set by the Authority.[42]

As of March 1957, the New York City Housing Authority was the landlord for 28,184 Negro families. The housing it provided was always physically superior to alternative available accommodations, although it has been troubled by problems of maintenance and deterioration and by the obligation of making places for a relatively large number of problem cases. Although there have been some difficulties in maintaining patterns of integrated living, the net effect of the expansion of public housing in New York City since the war has been advantageous to the nonwhite families in the region.[43]

The drawbacks in the public housing program have come largely from the reluctance of whites to move into neighborhoods identified as colored. Projects built in Negro ghettos have been almost totally Negro tenanted.[44] While the shift of low-income Negroes from a ghetto to public housing unit in a predominantly white area has advanced integration, new apartments subsidized by government funds in a colored district have only resulted in the passage of low-income Negro families from one ghetto to another.

The dislocated low-income Negro families which have not found places in public housing have been much less fortunate. Many have been displaced by new private housing, by schools, and by other public and office buildings. Little is known of their fate. But the law placed a responsibility for relocation on the sponsors of public, semipublic, or publicly assisted private projects; and the comprehensive Tenant Relocation Report of 1954 revealed the imposing difficulties even in those areas. The site clearance activities since 1945 created "an enforced population displacement completely unlike any previous population movement in the city's history." [45]

Some 63,630 tenant families, approximately 170,000 persons, had to leave their dwellings to make way for new projects between January 1, 1946, and March 31, 1953. Of those thus forced to move, fully 37 per cent were nonwhite and Puerto Rican, these groups constituting but 12.7 per cent of the city's population in 1950.[46] A rough estimate would place the number of displaced Negroes in New York in those seven years at 35,000 to 40,000 persons; and many more have had to move as a result of construction since then.

The families involved were definitely in the low-income category; only one-quarter of them earned over $3,500 a year. Only about 29 per cent of these people were relocated in public housing projects. The remainder had to find their own housing as best they could. The requirement that they be transferred to decent, safe, and sanitary dwellings was often ignored. Negroes more often than whites were forced into quarters as squalid as those they had left. They moved from slum ghetto to slum ghetto. Any improvement was a product not of planning but either of luck or of the general thinning out of the neighborhoods in which they lived.[47]

The immediate future of the low-income Negro family unable to qualify for, or to find accommodations in, public housing is far from encouraging. The ever-increasing Puerto Rican population will compete with the Negroes for the available units. New building does not help such families. Even with some governmental subsidy the private builder can just barely afford to build at less than $50.00 a room, a price out of reach of the poor; and rising building costs and property taxes make this a bare minimum.

The "filter down" process may help; those more fortunate New Yorkers who rent or buy new housing may ease the rental situation in areas they leave. But such relief can be expected only slowly and only if the migration out of the city proper continues heavy; for the volume of new building in the five boroughs has been relatively low. Only in the peak year of 1949 did residential construction at all rental ranges exceed 40,000 units. The average for the seven-year period of 1946–1952 was 29,107 new units. At the same time, Negro and Puerto Rican population was increasing at a rate of approximately 45,000 persons per year. Compensation for the difference came from building in the Region outside the city; but the space made available by prosperous families who move to Westchester or Long Island trickles down to the Negroes of Harlem only slowly and indirectly.[48]

Furthermore, the substandard quality of much of the housing in the city makes even the limited gains by new construction deceptive. Since the Negroes are generally the last to enter the private housing market, they must accept what becomes available by the departure of whites who move elsewhere in the city or to a suburban area. Invariably this is the least desirable housing, much of it old and below the building code standards. By national criteria, which apply to rural as well as to urban areas and are therefore rather loose, there were 281,988 substandard dwelling units in the city in 1950 and dilapidation threatens to grow worse rather than better. Fully 49.1 per cent of the 2,302,675 units in the city were constructed prior to 1919, and 19 per cent prior to 1899. Age is not the sole cause of dilapidation, but it is a major cause; and it is therefore reasonable to assume that many more units will become substandard before very long.[49]

The immediate future thus promises the low-income Negro little assurance of relief. Some of the glamor has gone out of the public housing program and many of its original backers are apathetic to its support. The Urban Renewal concept embodied in the Act of 1954 is not directed at satisfying the needs of low-income families. There is little local consideration of any comprehensive plan of rehabilitation which might ease the situation until building catches up with demand. Some community organizations have been interested in the problem but their effectiveness has been limited by their inability to agree upon a program. The district planning boards instituted by Mayor Wagner when he was Borough President of Manhattan have struggled to better their communities and to encourage capital improvements. Their influence may stimulate rehabilitation and rebuilding programs in depressed areas, but they cannot themselves expect to cope with the whole problem.[50]

The mobility of the low-income Negro family in the region is not now nor will it be in the near future a matter of personal choice. Extremely severe limitations will continue to restrict their ability to choose their place of residence. Such people already devote a larger proportion of their total income to rent than do whites (24.5 per cent as against 18.8 per cent in 1954); and can expect no improvement by raising the share of their earnings they devote to housing. They must either remain crowded in their present dwellings or, if they are dislocated, inherit substandard housing elsewhere.[51]

There is some hope that, in the future, living conditions in the neighborhoods in which they presently cluster will show some measure of improvement. In some sections of Harlem, as earlier in the East Side, the gradual aging of the population and the shrinkage of the average size of households has produced a thinning-out process. The resultant decline in residential density may not in itself lead to more commodious accommodations for those who remain, but it will at least relieve some of the pressures of overcrowding.

Furthermore, it is altogether possible that the housing built in the 1920's for middle-income groups will, in many parts of the region, be gradually vacated as its occupants die out and their children move to new districts. Such quarters may then trickle down to groups with lower incomes. In the past, however, only those Negroes whose earnings have risen above the level of the mass of the unskilled have been able to take advantage of such opportunities. In the last analysis, therefore, the chief hope of the low-income nonwhite family is for some improvement in economic status.

But, since the prospect for such an improvement depends on access to education, which in turn depends upon neighborhood resources, the result is a circular pattern of relation which for the moment leaves the individual helpless. On the other hand, a breakthrough at any point opens the possibility of improvement in all three areas.

The mutual dependence of status, education, and housing is most clearly revealed in the patterns of movement, within the Region, of the middle-income Negro family; they vary significantly from those of the low-income family. At least some Negroes have the earning power to afford superior quarters yet are prevented from securing them by prejudice. Fully 2 per cent of the Negroes who earn over $5,000 live in substandard dwellings, and many more occupy quarters but slightly above that.[52]

Only recently have legal remedies become available. The decision in the Dorsey Case of 1949 long deprived colored people of relief against discrimination in private housing. Not until 1955 did state law effectively forbid their exclusion from publicly assisted projects; and not until the end of 1957 did the municipal Sharkey-Brown-Isaacs ordinance outlaw discrimination in other multiple-family dwellings. Although this measure may eradicate some of the overt forms of exclusion in the five boroughs, the bitter hostility to it of the real estate interests revealed that limitations upon the freedom of colored people to reside where they wish are likely to remain real both in the city and in the Region outside it. It is still difficult for those with incomes adequate to meet the cost to find housing appropriate to their status.[53]

The mobile Negro is influenced by essentially the same factors as the white when choosing a home, whether a house or an apartment. The available facilities for the education of his children, the amount of space, and the desirability of owning as against renting are the most important considerations. The suburban ranch-type dwelling is as attractive in the pages of *Tan* as in those of *Life*.[54]

But the Negro finds it far more difficult to buy a house than the white in the Region. To do so he must surmount a variety of obstacles. The cost of single-family dwellings is high and the problem of financing is particularly difficult for colored people, for it is often impossible to obtain the necessary mortgage no matter how secure it may be. The F.H.A. generally refuses to insure loans on a home for a Negro in a predominantly white neighborhood no matter what collateral may be offered.[55]

The mortgage money market has been gradually opening to Negroes and probably will continue to do so at an accelerated rate. The Carver Savings and Loan Association, founded in January 1949 by a group of Negro business and professional men, has granted over 1,500 mortgages totaling $12,000,000 in less than a decade. Its successful experience as mortgagee has not only made substantial funds available to Negroes but has made many general banks aware of the potentially large Negro market. Its favorable experience with Negro mortgagors has encouraged the Empire, the Harlem, the Bowery, and the Brevoort Savings Banks, among others, to adopt a more liberal attitude.[56] Nevertheless the Negro still cannot count on the same ease of financing his home as a white of comparable income.

A second deterrent to home ownership by Negroes has been the belief that they depreciate property when they move into a neighborhood. It will be difficult to shake that belief, which often seems substantiated by the fact that the readiest moves are into districts already on the decline, and which is sometimes stimulated by brokers eager for a rapid turnover.

There are scattered instances of Negroes who bought houses in previously lily-white areas with little trouble; and a study, although limited in scope, reveals that over two-thirds of a mobile group of colored people moved to neighborhoods which are at least 50 per cent white. That may reflect a trend, but hardly one general enough to be immediately significant.[57]

In addition to the external restraints, the Negro's own inhibitions limit his freedom of choice. The apprehensive Negro buyer has heard that houses are scarce and that most neighborhoods are closed to families of his color. He is reluctant to expose himself to the degradation associated with prejudice, and accepts living conditions below his financial capacity rather than become involved in the unpleasantness of a conflict.

The most significant steps toward interracial housing patterns, therefore, will probably take place in apartment living in New York City. There law and habits hostile toward discrimination are most likely to develop. Early attempts to foster mixed settlement such as the middle-income project of the Bowery Savings Bank were not very successful; they tended to become entirely Negro. More recent interracial experiments such as Morningside Gardens, in which the auspices of Columbia University offered a kind of guarantee of status, or the low-cost General Grant houses in which residents were carefully chosen, have been more promising. But the areas of genuine open occupancy remain relatively small.[58]

An integrated housing pattern nevertheless remains the acknowledged goal both of the Negro and the general community. The Sharkey-Brown-Isaacs law may have some effect upon private dwellings; and the continuing efforts of the New York City Housing Authority to improve race relations may influence the character of the occupancy of its projects. The Urban League has sought to stimulate Negroes to cross over the boundaries of segregation by seeking quarters in white neighborhoods; and there are occasional signs that such penetration by individuals is accepted by those among whom they settle. At present, some 120,000 families are living in harmony in public, private, and cooperative homes in the five boroughs. That will also be the most likely point of change in the suburbs.[59]

But even those whites who welcome a pattern of diversity in housing are conscious of the desire about them for an "established community pattern" that guarantees "a congenial neighborhood in which congeniality is an index of security." [60] The longing for uniformity must be taken into account in any effort to mitigate the hardships for the Negroes that result from it. The resultant problems are most evident in the suburbs.

The tendency toward the dispersal of industry in the periphery of the Region has created numerous job opportunities in the outer ring of settlement. Negroes have found considerable openings for employment in these districts; and the Negro population of such urban centers as Newark and Mt. Vernon has grown rapidly. But thus far that has not led to the development of substantial colored suburban communities in Westchester, Long Island, or New Jersey. A very large percentage of those who work on the outskirts continue to commute from the center, in a reverse current to the dominant tide which daily flows inward from the suburbs to the central city.

In part, that is due to the fact that proximity to the place of employment is not yet a very weighty consideration in the determination of Negroes to move.[61] It is, however, also due to the fact that those who do shift their residences have generally been compelled either to accept places in existing Negro ghettos or to face special problems in locating themselves in predominantly white neighborhoods.

The old Negro settlements in Newark, Jersey City, and the smaller New Jersey and Long Island towns were always segregated and confined to the poorest available housing. Such communities often also had inherited an irksome tradition of master-servant relation. They have attracted from Manhattan primarily those families willing to accept accommodations but slightly better than those they left.[62]

However, most Negro families who can afford to buy homes do not wish to move out of the city in order to end up in a ghetto but little better than that of Harlem. Like their counterparts, they seek the dignity of property ownership, space, and better education.

In the suburbs they encounter physical and social barriers. There is little good low-cost housing there; and they must seek to penetrate as individuals rather than in a concentrated group. That leads to a clash of ideals between the desire of the whites for homogeneity and the aspiration of Negroes for equality. The attitude of members of non-Negro groups is partly negative; they fear that deterioration invariably accompanies the Negro. But it is also positive in that it values neighborhood homogeneity. On the other hand, the Negroes fear that no purely colored neighborhood will maintain its status as long as color is a sign of inferiority. The result is a continuing strain between Negro and intergroup agencies which push toward integration and homeowner and real estate groups which resist it.[63] The tension will persist so long as segregation is involuntary and lowers the status of those discriminated against by it.

Yet inevitably some part of the colored population will have to find a place in the suburbs. The only question is whether the move will come peacefully or be accompanied by ugly conflicts.

There are grounds for optimism on this account. If the barriers created by prejudice are relaxed and individuals become free to find the quality of housing they wish where they like, it is altogether possible that a gradual shift of Negro families into previously white neighborhoods will ease existing apprehensions and improve relations between the old and the new groups.[64] Under those conditions, there is no reason to suppose that the Negroes will be thoroughly dispersed throughout the region, any more than other ethnic groups are. Rather it is to be expected that common interests will lead to the development of Negro communities which are as coherent as those of the Irish, Jews, or Italians and which offer a variety of types of accommodations without the stigma of inferiority. In the study of the motives for Negro movement, not one respondent suggested that an integrated neighborhood was in itself an attraction and relatively few gave that factor any weight at all.[65] The regrouping of the Negro community, in which the well-to-do become as eager to preserve property values and disassociate themselves from the poor as their white counterparts, indicates that this would provide a more satisfactory basis for adjustment.[66] Examination of situations in which Negroes have been relieved of the anxiety of inferiority reveals that they are as prone as other groups to clannishness or self-segregation.[67] When the Long Island and Bergen Expressways, the New York Thruway, the Narrows Bridge, and other improvements in the next few years make additional space available and relieve the existing shortage of vacant land, there need be less reason for clash in the suburbs.[68]

The Puerto Ricans have followed a development analogous to that of the Negroes. Some of them had already been troubled by the problems of slum life on the island; and they found no relief in migration. Arriving later than the Negroes, they found the housing situation in New York already difficult. The earliest immigrants were cigar makers who settled on Cherry Street in the East Side, where there has since been a small colony. But there was no room to expand there. Instead the Puerto Ricans of the 1920's and 1930's moved to the edge of Harlem in space not pre-empted by the Negroes; the nucleus of settlement there was on Third Avenue at 101st Street. Bounded on the north by the Negroes, on the east by Italians, and on the south by a high rent district, they could only expand to the west. Before the war they had filtered along 110th Street to Morningside Heights. A somewhat smaller settlement also developed in the Navy Yard district of Brooklyn.[69]

The Harlem region was undesirable not only because of the low quality of its housing, which was often worse than that back on the island, but also because it tended to establish an identification with the Negroes that the Puerto Ricans did not particularly like.[70] Yet, when their numbers expanded, during and after the war, they found other parts of the city closed to them by the shortage of residential space, a shortage made more severe by slum clearance and the development of new housing projects. The early Brooklyn settlement, for instance, was thus completely displaced. They spread finally to the upper West Side of Manhattan, and thence southward as far down as 50th Street. The number in the lower East Side also grew; and colonies appeared in Bushwick in Brooklyn and in the East

Bronx where there were apartment houses susceptible to conversion. Their distribution by boroughs thus still reflects the restrictions upon their dispersal.[71]

The Puerto Ricans could, however, afford even these quarters only at the expense of a radical deterioration of standards. It is irrelevant to seek to locate the blame for that deterioration either on the rapacity of the landlords or the slothfulness of the tenants. The Puerto Rican slums of New York were the same in character as earlier immigrant slums. Like their predecessors, the Puerto Ricans were handicapped in the quest for housing by the fact that they were newcomers; and they were at a particular disadvantage because of the character of the postwar period in which they arrived.

The shortage of housing since 1940 and government policy combined to create a situation of considerable hardship for these people. The rent laws, which protected entrenched low-income groups, made the situation of recent arrivals worse, as landlords often found it possible to increase their incomes only by converting their properties into furnished flats or quasi-hotels. Frequently, therefore, the Puerto Ricans had no alternative but to accept subdivided apartments or furnished rooms at exhorbitant prices, taking in lodgers to make up the cost. The poor housing in the Bronx thus became worse; and the apartments of the West Side which had often been good were downgraded. The fortunate families able to find places in public housing escaped some of the worst problems. But the majority were squeezed into marginal dwellings by their own lack of choice and the rising value of real estate.[72]

For them too the suburbs have been attractive. They too would like to move for the advantages better neighborhoods would give their children. But thus far their growing numbers have been accommodated primarily by the spread of existing areas of settlement. It is true that the eagerness to find improved housing has contributed to the steady decline in the percentage of those who reside in Manhattan. But, until now, those who have left the area of initial settlement have done so primarily to go to the adjacent boroughs and to such industrial centers as Newark where some 12,800 found homes by 1959. But outside the city limits, in neighborhoods of more desirable housing, the Puerto Ricans have, no doubt, met obstacles similar to those encountered by the Negroes. To what extent those have been surmounted is hard to say, because of the special relation of the Puerto Ricans to color prejudice.[73]

Color complicated the problem of mobility for the Puerto Ricans and also made it difficult to trace their movements. The shock of discovering the significance of discrimination on the mainland created a marked temptation among the whites to sever their ties with the group. Many seized whatever opportunity they could to move away to neighborhoods where they would not be known as Puerto Ricans. The colored, on the other hand, stressed their identification with the group as a means for keeping themselves apart from the Negroes. It seems likely therefore that the spread has been greater than is apparent, for the individuals most likely to move are also those most likely to lose themselves in the general community.

It seems safe to predict that, although both the Negro and Puerto Rican groups will grow in size, most of that growth will come outside the original centers of settlement in Manhattan. A useful estimate is that less than 10 per cent of growth in the next two decades will be in that borough, with the remainder divided between the other four boroughs and the outer cities of the suburban counties. The more important question is whether that will come peacefully or as a result of a disruptive struggle.

Housing difficulties are both symptomatic of and contributory to many other problems of social adjustment. The degree of success in resolving them will not only influence access to education, to occupational opportunities, and to rising status, but also the general health of the whole community. Housing poor enough to create slum conditions also has a relation—although not a precisely definable one—to social delinquency. Hence the bitterness of the conflicts over living space.

An examination of the social adjustment of the Puerto Ricans and Negroes must take account both of the tensions around them and the effect of an undesirable environment. By habit and tradition New Yorkers have been unwilling to acknowledge either that they have allowed themselves unjustly to discriminate against some of the residents of their city or that certain disorders are inherent in the situations of urban life. They are particularly reluctant to do so now, when a large percentage of them are the children and grandchildren of immigrants who themselves suffered from the debilitating effects of settlement in slums.

Instead, the community, whether in 1820 or 1890 or 1957, has attempted to justify itself by arguing that broken families, illegitimacy, disease, criminality, prostitution, juvenile delinquency, insanity, and pauperism were the products of the backwardness of the particular groups among whom these phenomena were manifested. It is necessary to search beneath that justification to arrive at a proper assessment of the adjustment of the Negroes and Puerto Ricans to the terms of New York life.

Two related propositions—which can be proven—will clear the ground for more profitable discussion: first, that some degree of social disorder has been an inescapable concomitant of all American urban growth whatever the population involved; and, second, that no asocial traits or deficiencies of intelligence inherent in the character of the Negroes or the Puerto Ricans makes those people delinquent.[74] Accepting those propositions, it is possible to pose two meaningful questions: first, has the effect of the Negro and Puerto Rican migration been to raise the rates of social disorder in the metropolitan region; and, second, are the Negroes and Puerto Ricans in the New York situation more susceptible to these disorders than other groups?

The answer to the first question is almost certainly negative. The data do not readily lend themselves to comparisons across time, but in only one area, that of mental illness, do they point to significant deterioration; and that may reflect rather the growth in the means of detecting and providing institutional care for sufferers than an actual increase. More to the point, comparisons with other cities which have not experienced the immigration of Puerto Ricans and Negroes, show that New York has not suffered disproportionately from any of these disorders. Whatever qualifications and refinements may have to be made in presenting these materials, they certainly do not support the contention that the effect of immigration has been deleterious. The most that can be said is that such social disorders have generally accompanied the growth of large urban centers, no matter what population was involved; these are part of the social cost of developing metropolitan cities like New York.[75]

It is more difficult to answer the second question. The available statistical data must be accepted with many reservations. It is biased against the Negro and Puerto Ricans, people who are more likely than others to come to public attention and to require public care in illness, death, crime, and delinquency. Most of the figures are further distorted, in their implications at least, because they make simple comparisons between whites and nonwhites or Puerto Ricans as if the whites were an entirely unified and homogeneous group. Thus an interesting Youth Board study of juvenile delinquency treats the non-Puerto Rican whites as an entity although in respect to this problem there are probably marked differences among the Irish, Italians, and Jews thrust together in this category.[76]

With these reservations in mind, it is possible to conclude only that the Negroes and Puerto Ricans show a somewhat higher rate of delinquency than the whole of the rest of the population. But they may not be uniformly more delinquent than other particular ethnic groups.

The most useful light on the reasons for delinquency emerges from recent studies of the differentials in the health of the various segments of the city's population. These data seem more accurate than most; and within them the various ethnic groups are treated more carefully. Negroes and Puerto Ricans seem to show a greater susceptibility to mental and physical illness than other whites. In part, that must be due to the unfavorable heritage they brought with them from the lands of their birth where tuberculosis and other diseases, although declining, were still almost endemic.[77] The difficulties of migration no doubt further weakened their capacity to resist. But the high rates of tuberculosis and of venereal disease seem also related to the conditions of their settlement in New York. There is a clear relation between slum life and these disorders.[78]

Yet not all these disorders can be explained simply in terms of environment and antecedents, important as those factors are. Although both the Negroes and Puerto Ricans have suffered from the unfavorable effects of migration and poor housing, the latter have shown greater capacity for physical adaptation. Their mortality rate is not excessive by comparison with other whites, while that of the Negroes is measurably higher. Furthermore, the general incidence of disease seems lower and the level of health higher among Puerto Ricans than among the Negroes.[79]

Two additional factors enter into the explanation of the differential. A careful study of the incidence of mental disease shows the importance of migration and of recency of arrival, factors that would apply to both groups. But the same analysis also reveals that movement from within the United States was more likely to be a source of disorder than movement from outside it.[80] These findings may be related to those of a perceptive investigation of the elements influencing the health of a sample of New York Puerto Rican families. That analysis demonstrated that, beyond the physical and environmental factors, the extent to which the social milieu helped the individual define goals that made his life worth while was a significant element in determining the degree to which he could maintain a healthy existence.[81]

It seems possible to conclude from such data that the deviations of both groups, and the wider deviations of the Negroes, are due to the forces that weaken their sense of purpose in life—to the shock of migration with its attendant disruption of family authority, to low economic conditions and slum life, and to the feebleness of internal communal institutions which deprive these groups of control and discipline. The greater susceptibility of the Negroes to delinquency could thus be accounted for by the fact that all the elements that tended to sap their sense of purpose were more extreme than in the case of the Puerto Ricans. Migration was also a sharper divide in the lives of the latter; and they were, furthermore, less limited by color in the range of opportunities for social advancement, for desirable housing, and for education.

This analysis is confirmed by the evidence on the incidence of juvenile delinquency, criminality, and other disorders. The data of juvenile delinquency are notoriously difficult to handle. The statistics, even for arrests, are not altogether reliable; and there is a good deal of uncertainty about what they measure, since they are inconsistent in the identification of what delinquency consists of and are biased against the poor and against ethnic minorities. It is improbable that one could derive from them valid generalizations concerning long-term trends in the metropolitan region.[82]

Most contemporary impressions focus upon those forms of delinquency expressed in gang behavior. But this is not the whole or, perhaps, even the most important aspect of the problem. At any given time in the past decade, there seem to have been, in the city, fewer than one hundred juvenile gangs involving not more than 8,000 youths between the ages of fifteen and seventeen. Such of them as had a formal structure were not purely ethnic, but reflected the characteristics of the neighborhoods in which they operated. Negro and Puerto Rican youngsters have frequently been drawn into them, but also those of Irish or Italian antecedents. Essentially they seem hardly different from the gangs of pre-Civil War New York.[83]

But gang behavior is not the typical expression of delinquency, which involves more often nonviolent infractions of the law or incorrigible family behavior.[84] With regard to this wider area, there is no evidence of a noticeable increase in the gravity of the problem since the arrival of the Negroes and the Puerto Ricans. At most one can conclude from existing data that in the past forty years there has been a cyclical movement in the volume of delinquency that correlates positively with periods of prosperity and of war and the threat of war. Even that must be qualified by the necessity for taking account of the changes in definition introduced by the Young Act of 1948. Still more tentatively, one may assert that there has been some shift in the character of delinquency since 1945 with the spread in the use of narcotics and of firearms. But this may well be a result of tendencies toward violence general to postwar social behavior rather than peculiar to any age or ethnic group.[85]

Negroes and Puerto Ricans form a substantial part of the population of the eleven areas marked out by the Youth Board as those with the highest incidence of delinquency; and its experimental study as of 1956 showed that those groups were more likely to fulfill expectations of delinquency than "whites." Yet, both the Herlands report of 1943 and the Board of Education report of 1952, as well as an earlier study of the situation in 1930, found only a slight correlation between delinquency and poverty, minority status, or inadequate housing and recreational facilities.[86]

Whatever excessive susceptibility the Negroes and Puerto Ricans show toward delinquency is more closely related to failures of personal adjustment. There is no unanimity of opinion among students of the subject about the etiology of delinquency; but the most persuasive theories share a common view of the social situation of the delinquent. Whether the specific cause of breakdown be attributed to disrupted families, intergenerational conflict, personal anxieties and frustrations, or the influence of the peer group and the mass media, these explanations reveal the delinquent as an individual unsure of his own intentions and defiant of the authority that sustains values unacceptable or inadequate to his own life.[87]

The vulnerability of Negro and Puerto Rican youth is altogether comprehensible in those terms. The fictional treatment of the problem puts a convincing emphasis on these themes. Boys and girls are depicted as driven to delinquency by deprivation, family conflict, the desire to hurt unsympathetic parents, and the conviction that the adult world was hostile and its rules irrelevant. Children incapable of accepting the values of the world, as the consciousness of prejudice dawned upon them, were most likely to conclude "I'm already messed up, why shouldn't I mess up?" [88]

The degree to which young people in these groups will, in the future, yield to delinquency will certainly be influenced by the extent to which they will come to find the standards of the community relevant to their own lives. But the problem will not disappear of itself. In fact, as the number of juveniles between the ages of five and twenty increases in the years to come, after its decline between 1930 and 1950, these difficulties may become socially more burdensome than ever before.

The identical convergence of forces also leads some members of these groups to criminality. The rate of arrests of Puerto Ricans seems somewhat higher than that of other whites; and that of Negroes is higher still. But the difference is not excessive and is explicable in terms of factors analogous to those involved in juvenile delinquency. The temptation to defy a hostile society, represented by the police and the law, and the belief, whether ill-founded or not, that the police are especially brutal in the treatment of minorities, account for whatever differences may exist.[89]

When it comes to other disorders, the incidence among Negroes and Puerto Ricans may not be excessive; but the high degree of visibility of these groups and their readiness to seek the aid of government agencies may exaggerate the extent of their deviations. The common impression, for instance, that they form an undue percentage of the cases on the relief rolls has given rise to the belief that these people readily become dependent, although careful studies have shown that the number who seek public assistance is not larger than might be expected in view of their economic and social status.[90]

With reference to still other forms of delinquency, the incidence among Puerto Ricans and Negroes may not be significantly greater than in other segments of the population, but violations of the law are not regarded within the group with the moral disapprobation attached to them in the wider community. Neither the Negroes nor the Puerto Ricans see any ethical deficiencies in gambling; and they accept policy and its associated rackets as a matter of course. If the numbers game is regarded as an evil at all, it is a necessary one that plays a useful part in the lives of men and women for whom advancement is more a dream than a possible reality. But the long history of gambling in the city and its prevalence among other groups shows that what is different is the form and the open acceptance rather than the extent of participation.[91]

Only in the addiction to narcotics and in sexual disorders do these groups seem to supply an unusual number of offenders, although here too that judgment must be qualified by the possibility that an acquiescent attitude that openly recognizes deviants may account for some part of the apparent excess. The general growth in the traffic in drugs has put them within reach of a relatively large sector of the population which seeks in them an escape comparable to that which other people find in alcoholism. And the number of illegitimacies and abortions, the frequency of homosexuality and sex crimes, and the generally lax attitude toward sexual behavior is certainly related to the chaotic family life prevalent in these groups.[92]

Disorganized family relations thus enter into many aspects of the social disorders that trouble the Negroes and Puerto Ricans of New York, as they did earlier immigrants. Even in advance of their departure from the places of their birth the members of both groups suffered from the instability of home life, and the strain became more intense in the course of migration and resettlement. The frequency of consensual unions and the casual standards of sexual behavior in both groups sap the strength of family ties. In addition, the Negroes must cope with ancient scars inherited from slavery and the Puerto Ricans with the effects of the inability to transplant the traditional Hispano-Catholic courtship system or extended kinship patterns. In both groups, the woman's role as a wage-earner and the second-generation child's aggressiveness weaken the man's authority as husband and father.[93]

In the context of poverty and slum life, the instability of the family becomes a pervasive source of personal disorder. The individual on the verge of trouble seeks in vain for support from the security of fixed relationships as child or parent, husband or wife. Deprived also of external control or discipline from strong ethnic institutions and prevented, by intruding fears of color, from accepting fully the standards of the broader American community, such an individual is likely to yield to a sense of isolation and through one form of delinquency or another to strike back at the hostile society to which he remains a stranger. At the crises, which an adverse life situation makes frequent, when a Negro or Puerto Rican feels adrift, without a clear sense of purpose or goals, he has no props to lean upon and is the easy victim of disaster. Any accident is a catastrophe to which the only possible reaction is collapse which among Puerto Ricans may take the form of an emotional *ataque,* among Negroes, of a sullen desperation.[94]

The failures of adjustment were thus only in part products of the process by which strangers were transplanted to an urban setting. They were also derived from weaknesses peculiar to the situation of Negroes and Puerto Ricans. Enjoying more limited opportunities for advancement and mobility than did their predecessors and without communal institutions or leadership adequate to their needs, these people were especially vulnerable to the dangers of the city.

There is a genuine, and ominous, possibility that they will remain so in the future. If they do, the people of the New York Metropolitan Region will have to meet the calamitous social costs created by the actual and potential delinquency of a large part of the population. And, paradoxically, the greatest danger may emerge outside the central city, where the municipal authorities are at least aware of the problem and where voluntary social agencies have had more than a century's experience in dealing with it. But the outlying communities, unequipped by tradition or history to deal with such questions and inclined to believe that they do not really exist, may find themselves suddenly overwhelmed by the consequences.

But there is also a prospect for improvement, although it will take more than slum clearance or the expansion of recreational facilities to make it real. It will take, in addition, the steady elimination of the abnormalities in the situation of the Negroes and Puerto Ricans. When color and ethnic identity cease to be unbearable burdens, when opportunity for jobs, education, and housing becomes genuinely equal, and when the family acquires a measure of stability, the Negroes and Puerto Ricans will at least have a firm base upon which to construct a sound communal life. Then one may expect a significant abatement in the rates of delinquency.

Whether the development of the future moves in one direction or the other will depend on the people of the city. They will have to choose whether these newest arrivals are to be welcomed as equals or treated as enemies, whether they are to be given seats in the same schools and apartments in the same houses or excluded as foes to the existing order—which they will then become. Much hangs on the character of that choice.

5
Forms of Social Action

The strains of a difficult transition have left their marks upon the Negroes and Puerto Ricans, as upon the earlier groups who settled in the City. In the case of all such people, the ability to develop an adjustment that would assure the individuals involved a healthy creative life depended both on the nature of the hurdles to be surmounted and on the resources available for doing so. The hardships of the Negroes and the Puerto Ricans arise from the fact that the hurdles are unusually high and the resources unusually meager.

In the character of their communal life, the Negroes and Puerto Ricans are farthest removed from the experiences of earlier immigrant groups. They do, of course, find outlets for conviviality, gossip, friendship, and sporadic mutual aid in family and neighborhood cliques.[1] But these latest additions to New York's population have not developed the integrated pattern of voluntary organizations that gave their predecessors understanding of the problems of metropolitan life and aid in dealing with them.

It was significant, for instance, that the array of hospitals, orphanages, homes for the aged, and other philanthropic institutions established and supported by the nineteenth-century immigrants had no counterpart among the Negroes or Puerto Ricans. As a result, they could not find the help they needed within the context of the group; and the group lacked this means of giving its identity significant expression.

These people have also been slow to develop other media through which to communicate with one another and arrive at an understanding of their place in society. The facilities which have appeared spontaneously are poorly and inadequately led. The streets of Harlem offer them saloons and coffee shops for gathering places; and, for entertainment, night clubs, dance halls, and movie houses that specialize in Spanish films. In both groups, amateur and semiprofessional theaters have only just begun to take form. The lesser radio and television stations direct at them occasional programs of music and community news. WHOM has a variety of Spanish language programs, including lessons in English and advice on practical problems. *The Amsterdam News,* a weekly, is directed at the Negroes and *La Prensa* supplies the Puerto Ricans with the services of a daily newspaper, while *El Diario de Nueva York* caters to the tastes of tabloid readers. The string of Johnson magazines published in Chicago has a substantial market among New York Negroes and satisfies the taste for sensationalism, sex, and athletics in pictures and stories.

But all these publications have also made a significant beginning in the coverage of communal news and comment. They make some room for popular and serious literature. They offer counsel on family and labor difficulties and attempt to develop a rapport with their readers that may grow more important in the future. As yet, however, they do not supply an equivalent to the cultural and social resources available to earlier groups at a comparable state of settlement.[2]

Other social organizations have been slow to take form. The Puerto Ricans had considerable trade union experience on the island and there are Spanish-speaking locals in some unions. But their leaders are inherited from other groups; and many of their unions have acquired the reputation of being rackets, linked to the underworld. Only among the Pullman car porters, who won recognition in 1935, has labor organization really fallen within group lines, as it did for the Irish, Jews, or Italians fifty years earlier. Fraternal organizations have somewhat more significance but have relatively low memberships. Among the Negroes these activities are focused in the lodges. Among the Puerto Ricans, since 1950, there has been a proliferation of societies—many based on the locality of origin in the island—and also some effort at confederation and at practical social work.[3]

Among the Negroes, only the churches have genuine vitality and influence. These institutions reach back to the early past of the group in the United States, they are independent of white control, and they offer a medium for the intimate display of feelings. Into them can be projected all sorts of mystical longings for security and belonging, for faith healing, and for assurance against the obliteration by death. They thus supply a deep emotional need and seem to establish ties between the individual and a meaningful larger communion. Furthermore, the wider society nowadays not only approves of all religion as a good thing in itself, but also recognizes the validity of this type of difference in identification, so that the separateness of the Negro churches is not a sign of their inferiority. The desire for some religious affiliation draws colored people not only into the branches of the major Protestant denominations, but also into a multitude of store-front churches and into sects like Jehovah's Witnesses and the colored "Jews" and "Moslems" which minimize race distinctions.[4]

The Puerto Ricans have been attracted in the same direction, although more slowly. They were Catholics at their arrival but tended to be lax and apathetic, partly from habits acquired on the island, where the great majority of the population were negligent in observance, and partly from the influence of their loyalist sympathies during the Spanish civil war. In any case the church here seemed alien to them, dominated as it was by Irish and Italians. Only La Milagrosa seemed distinctively Puerto Rican, even a decade ago.[5]

More recently, however, there have been indications of a growing interest in a return to the traditional faith. Church-affiliated organizations, such as the Daughters of Mary and the Knights of Columbus, have begun to attract Spanish-speaking members. Even more interesting has been the rapid spread of Protestantism; Puerto Rican newspaper advertisements regularly list Sunday services in Baptist, Episcopal, Evangelical, Methodist, Pentecostal, and Presbyterian, as well as in Catholic churches. The Pentecostal sects have been popular, as among the Negroes, because of their indulgence of emotionalism, superstition, and charms. But, as among the Negroes, they have also given frightened men and women reassurance that a personal Deity was available to assist them against the perils of illness, the pains of death, and the difficulties of life. A few also see religion primarily as a social institution, part of the pattern of Americanization; such people, while they may themselves remain atheists or unaffiliated, send their children to some church as a means of furthering their adjustment to the expectations of the wider society.[6]

The trend last mentioned may have greater significance in the future. Until recently the church, among both groups, was the means through which they sought compensation for their deprivations and exclusion from the good things of society. For a few, at least, it is now becoming one of the signs of acceptance by that society.

Giving due regard to what has actually developed, it is still true that the Negroes and Puerto Ricans have not matched the richness and breadth of the communal life of the earlier immigrants.

Poverty alone was not enough to explain the difference. Although these people occupied the lowest level of the occupational hierarchy they were no worse off than the eastern and southern European immigrants of fifty years ago. Indeed, the prosperity of the period since 1940 actually gave the Negroes and Puerto Ricans an earning power superior to that of their predecessors, both in actual and relative terms. That comparative well-being provided them with the means that might have been used to develop a rich associational life had they wished to do so.

They did not. Complex reasons generated among them a sense of apathy toward communal organization that has played an important part in shaping the character of their adjustment.

For neither the Negroes nor the Puerto Ricans was the break of migration to New York as sharp as it had been for Europeans. The Italian or the Polish Jew who came to New York in 1907 knew that he had decisively severed his ties with his old home, that he would not return, and that his future was entirely in the United States. Furthermore, as an alien who felt detached from the life around him, he was sensitive to the obligation of creating his own instruments of social action.

By contrast, the Negroes and Puerto Ricans were American citizens; and that diminished the distance between Harlem on the one hand and Mississippi or the island on the other. Migration was not the decisive break it had been for the Europeans. The movement of individuals back and forth between the old home and the new never ceased, so that communications were close and the sense of connectedness was never broken. In this respect the Negroes and the Puerto Ricans were similar to the French-Canadians of New England and the Mexicans of the Southwest who were also never altogether detached from the lands of their birth. Such newcomers did not feel the complete and total sense of foreignness that overwhelmed the European immigrants and, therefore, did not feel called upon to create the institutions which were the response to the shock of separation.

The sense of connectedness also made them receptive to the influence of the mass media which were in any case growing enormously in importance in the years of the arrival in the city. They quickly became listeners to the radio and watchers of television; and they responded to the attractiveness of Hollywood movies. Before long they took to reading the *News* and *Mirror* and before long they learned to go dancing downtown at the Palladium or out at Hunt's Point Palace in preference to Laurel Gardens close to home. Before long, too, the newspapers or means of entertainment peculiar to the group became ancillary rather than central to their lives. The extent to which Negroes and Puerto Ricans had turned to the general press was revealed during the newspaper strike of 1958, when the circulation of *El Diario* and the *Amsterdam News* doubled. There may have been some non-Puerto Rican whites among the readers who turned to these papers for want of alternative; but by far the largest percentage of them were Negroes and Puerto Ricans who in more normal times bought the *News* or *Mirror* each morning. In any case, even the pages of the groups' own journals revealed the penetrating power of the mass media for they contained listings of the downtown theaters, comics such as Blondie but thinly disguised as Pepita, Amy Vanderbilt on etiquette, and Dorothy Dix on the problems of love.[7]

The mass media by their very nature were incapable of supplying the peculiar needs of the members of these ethnic groups. Group consciousness did not subside; it was fed from other sources. But it lacked appropriate means of articulation and expression; and that further inhibited the development of ethnic communal life.

The times were also discouraging. The prominence of the segregation issue made the goal of integration all-encompassing. Any separate institution bore the imputation of inferiority and the taint of Jim Crow; and the strategy of the struggle against discrimination, as in the case of hospitals and schools, seemed to demand a rejection of any mode of action in which Negroes and Puerto Ricans were set off as groups. It seemed preferable to accept the facilities of agencies created by the earlier, departing residents of the neighborhoods they occupied.

In a sense, too, the need for some of the traditional philanthropic services declined as responsibility for them shifted from voluntary to governmental agencies. After 1933, the welfare state assumed many social obligations earlier immigrants had borne themselves; it seemed pointless then to duplicate its activities.

Both the Puerto Ricans and the Negroes yielded readily to that tendency. Neither brought with them a tradition of philanthropy or communal solidarity. Some Negroes indeed had become accustomed to a role as recipients of aid; and, in the absence of voluntary associations on the island, many Puerto Ricans had learned to look for help to the efficient agencies of the commonwealth government which retained a long-term interest in their future. Many still maintain contact with the office of the Puerto Rican Department of Labor established in New York since 1930. As a result neither the Negroes nor the Puerto Ricans were inclined, in order to create their own institutions, to struggle against the trend, since the depression, toward the reliance upon the state. Indeed, the latter group, at least, was prone to regard government action as desirable even in their personal lives. Thus it seemed almost a matter of course that the Sydenham Hospital, once it was integrated, should shift from voluntary to municipal control.[8]

The lack of leadership was associated with the slowness of communal development both as a cause and a result. The low rate of social mobility limited the growth in numbers of the intellectuals and professional or business people who became the leaders of other ethnic groups. What was more, in the case of the Puerto Ricans, the incentive to pass, the advantages gained by those who could dissolve their ties to the group, further weakened the potential for leadership. Many who rose felt no sense of responsibility for the group as a whole and were resented and disliked by those who could not rise.

Negroes and Puerto Ricans willing and able to exercise creative leadership have consequently been tragically rare. Their place was taken rather by interpreters—in the literal or figurative sense—characters who used their slightly larger knowledge of the wider society to mediate between it and the ethnic group, often in their own interest. Such men were too weak and too timid to initiate action; often they merely accepted the values of the dominant "American" whites. On the other hand, the absence of communal institutions deprived other elements among them of the opportunity for training in leadership.[9]

The weakness of Negro communal institutions is reflected in the character of its Society. The efforts of an elite upper group to define itself go back to the late nineteenth century. But the result was, and still is, entirely derivative from and imitative of its image of white Society. The very wealthiest colored people aspire to move to country estates; and some of them have acquired mansions in Irvington, Hastings-on-Hudson, Tarrytown, and elsewhere in Westchester. They vacation in resorts like that at Oak Bluffs on Martha's Vineyard. They join social clubs like the Guardsmen and the Gentry that make an effort at exclusiveness, and they spend large sums on coming-out parties, debutante balls, formals, and benefits at "downtown" hotels like the Essex House, the Warwick, and the Belmont Plaza in mid-Manhattan and the St. George in Brooklyn.[10]

But this Society lacks a meaningful relation to the whole community and it is internally weak, incoherent, and incapable of maintaining its own standards. The elegant Delano Village cannot select its tenants well enough to avoid frequent evictions; and the social columns of the *Amsterdam News* remain open to an indiscriminate variety of persons.[11] The absence of strong communal institutions deprives this would-be elite of a functional role and leaves it detached from the mass of New York Negroes. Furthermore, it cannot hold the respect of a group all of whose members have a common background of slavery and service. In the last analysis, the inability to hold on to capital from generation to generation and the lack of a strong family tradition render Negro society unstable and permit newcomers with quick money—no matter how gained—or glamor readily to break in.[12]

Hence the importance among the Negroes of clergymen of a generally docile type. Hence too the opening for tragic demagoguery. The absence of responsible leadership in 1919, while colored people still reeled from the shock of their deteriorating position after the new migrations and after the frustration of their wartime hope, permitted Marcus Garvey to lead them off in futile pursuit of a nationalist fantasy. To this day small groups of Garveyites still hold their own in Harlem.[13] In the 1930's a similar vacuum made room for Father Divine's proffer of mystical relief from depression and prejudice.[14] And the more recent parallel of Adam Powell showed how little progress has been made; not many who saw through his use of the color issue as a blind were willing to oppose him.[15]

In the nature of the case, efforts to define a Puerto Rican Society have been even slower to develop and less consequential in their results. There is some feeling of distinctiveness on the part of the old settlers and the New York-born as against the more recent arrivals; and in the vacation resorts in the neighborhood of Newburgh, New York, there is a kind of meeting place for the more prosperous. But the group as a whole is too recent in its settlement to have developed strata of any degree of rigidity; and that tendency is further inhibited by the opportunities open to the most prosperous and least pigmented for passing out of the group entirely.[16]

For both the Negroes and the Puerto Ricans these problems are complicated by the difficulty of establishing the identity of the group. Among the latter there is some value to being known as Puerto Ricans, not only out of pride, but also because that designation differentiates them from the Negroes and also establishes their American citizenship. Yet concern about their suspected low reputation in the general community and the hostility of their neighbors—the Negroes, Italians, and Jews among whom they live—often leads them to shun a designation to which so many prejudices are attached. They sometimes use the circumlocution, *Boricua,* or, more often, emphasize the linguistic and cultural differences between themselves and other New Yorkers by referring to themselves as Latinos or Hispanos. Their organizations often bear in their titles the descriptive adjective, Spanish or Hispanoamericano or even Cuban-American; and Columbus Day, *el dia de la raza,* has become for them, as for the Italians, the symbol of belonging.[17]

The evasiveness of these usages is transparent, and particularly to the second generation which wishes at the same time to be American and yet to understand its own distinctiveness. Such people grope without much help toward an awareness of their identity. Sometimes they find it easier to escape entirely by passing. Often they are aroused to defensive group solidarity only in response to external attacks.[18]

The central problem of identification is settled for the Negroes by the fact that it is the white society that sets them apart as a group. For a long time, this enforced affiliation created the pathological attitude that assimilation was the only acceptable ideal and that passing was the ultimate although unattainable solution to the difficulties of the colored people.[19]

Traces still persist of the tendency to accept whiteness as the norm from which the black deviates. A debutante's ball is called the Snowball Cotillion; the makers of Black and White bleaching cream promise their customers lighter skins; nose- and hair-straightener advertisements still appear in the press; and there is a cocktail called, by an interesting conjunction, a white cadillac.[20] This submerged bias has entered into the preference among some for alternatives to the designation Negro, which range from African to Non-White. So too, an association of Jamaicans chose as its name, Londoners, Inc.[21]

At the same time, a consciousness of having been rejected leads some Negroes to a revulsion against the whole world of whiteness. Their fiction sometimes contains the titillating suggestion that intermarriage and passing are by their nature ill-omened and lead to retribution.[22] At its most extreme, that tendency generates African nationalism and even a hostility to Christianity as the product "of the so-called Negroes' enemies." [23]

In the ambiguity about their own identity in which so many Negroes and Puerto Ricans are trapped are the seeds of many frustrations. The lack of certainty about who they really are enters also into many running irritations in the course of daily life that seem to align one ethnic group against another; and it stimulates the inclination of both, as well as of the Italians, Jews, Irish, and "Americans" among whom they live, to believe that they are being persecuted by the others.[24]

Paradoxically, it is mostly when it is on the defensive that each group is sure of its identity. And, by the same token, it is on the formal level of "intergroup relations" that they are most effective in working together. Since the war and the reaction against the Hitlerite atrocities, no significant element in the city has openly defended race prejudice; and cooperation has become an imperative. Furthermore, in the effort to end discrimination and assure fair conditions of housing, employment, and education, all these people perceive common goals; and in the creation of conditions that will minimize conflict they perceive common interests that reflect their common conditions as minorities. And that basis of cooperation may prove increasingly significant in the future.

In the last decade, there have been encouraging signs of a change in two areas, politics and the struggle for equality. Action in these fields may supply a basis for more coherent communal organization in the future.

The major party machines were early aware of the potential of the

Negro vote and they have consistently tried to earn its support, even to the point of putting an occasional colored man in office. The Puerto Ricans also earned the attention of the professionals quickly. Congressman La Guardia was well aware of their presence in the 1920's and Vito Marcantonio made strenuous and successful efforts to cultivate them in the next decade.[25]

That has not changed. What has transformed apathy into involvement is the realization, or hope, that politics can be a means of effecting a fundamental improvement in their own situation. Earlier, even the Puerto Ricans who were familiar with American governmental processes were hesitant and skeptical about taking a personal part in politics. The Negroes, long accustomed to subordination, were even more so. Now increasingly they are persuaded that they can influence the election of officeholders and that the choices they make can have genuine significance in their lives. If these people are not disillusioned by successive frustrations, this may prove a significant incentive toward organization, particularly since government plays so important a part in their daily existence.[26]

That has already been the effect, among the Negroes, of the struggle for civil rights. At the start, the defensive associations, such as the Urban League and the N.A.A.C.P., were strongly influenced by whites and tended to overlook the utility of a mass following. But there has been a radical change since World War II as the awareness of being attacked heightened group consciousness and emphasized the need for common action. Equality ceased to be an abstraction and an unattainable ideal. It now became intimately related to the flat in which one lived, the job one held, and the school one's children attended. This concern has not only transformed the defense societies, it has also given a new seriousness to the press which is fond of emphasizing that, whatever the "daily paper" may say, "Your *Amsterdam News* is still with YOU!" As a result large numbers of the formerly disinterested have been drawn into social action.[27]

The Negroes are interested not only in the development of their rights in New York, but also in the struggle for desegregation in the South; that is a sign of their growing group consciousness. They avidly followed the Little Rock story and read with interest long accounts of news of violence or discrimination in the South. They know that whites can help and have an obligation to do so; thus an article on the slowness of the Yankees to take on Negro baseball players commented wryly that the team was "guided by a man with the fine old minority name of Weiss." [28] But they know also that in the last analysis they must depend on themselves; even the well-intentioned whites are likely to be victims of prejudice. The result is a growing sense of self-reliance. Indeed there is often an ironic attitude toward color; the moral of a story of a Brava white woman misclassified as colored for twenty-six years was: what difference did it make? [29]

A mounting sense of pride is characteristic of the new frame of mind. The Negro renaissance of the 1920's began the group's positive revaluation of itself; and that is constantly being stimulated by a sense of present accomplishment. There is much interest in the history and in the political, cultural, athletic, and economic achievements of the colored people.[30]

This pride is often extended from the group in the United States to all colored people throughout the world. This is no longer merely a matter of gratification at the award of Liberian decorations. It is more often a recognition of the solidarity of oppressed men fighting for freedom. News of Nigeria or Ghana is followed with great interest, for the struggle of such nations for independence is identified with the Negro struggle here for equality, as is the resistance to *apartheid* in South Africa.[31]

Somewhat more slowly than among the Negroes, there has been a recent development of both political awareness and group consciousness among the Puerto Ricans. The number who vote has increased as has the purposefulness with which they do so; and a few now have their sights fixed on a share of public office. The annual May 5 parade is regarded by some as a weapon in the fight for equality; for in it the Hispanos demonstrate their size, their voting and purchasing power, and their adaptability to American life. There is even talk of a "Spanish Party." Meanwhile the younger people have begun to form organizations out of which a community may develop. They too feel an interest in, and sympathy with, similar people elsewhere, in their case the Latin-Americans.[32]

Frustration and bitterness may convert this group feeling into a narrow, self-defeating hatred of the outsiders. There are demagogues among the Negroes and nationalist agitators among the Puerto Ricans ready to take advantage of such a turn of events. On the other hand, these communities can also evolve, as their predecessors did, into useful instruments of their members' adjustment to metropolitan life. There are signs that they are beginning to do so in the willingness of many social organizations to deal with such problems as juvenile delinquency and intergroup conflict in cooperation with government agencies, labor unions, and voluntary organizations.[33]

Although the difficulties are genuine and grave, there is every reason to be optimistic about the future, if the society of which these people have become a part allows them to act freely and as equals within it. If New York continues to witness, in the next twenty-five years as it has in the past decade, an abatement of prejudice in accord with its tradition of diversity, the problems of occupational mobility, of education, and of the competition for space will certainly be eased. Under such conditions, the differences that identify the Negroes and the Puerto Ricans will lose their stigmatizing effect and will become the basis for the healthy development of ethnic communities that will be a source of strength to their members. Values defined in such contexts will give meaning, order, and purpose to the lives of individuals and will be reflected back in improvements in education and in housing and in a liquidation of the most troubling social disorders. The whole Region will profit thereby.

Much depends on making this possibility a reality. The alternative in a democratic society is almost unthinkable.

6

Conclusion

In historical perspective, the Negroes and the Puerto Ricans in the New York Metropolitan Region do not present the radically new problem they seem to pose in the columns of the daily newspaper. Rather, their adjustment, difficult as it is, is but the most recent of a long series. The hardships such people have created and suffered have been concomitants of the necessity for accommodating in the city a large, unskilled, and poorly paid labor force needed for urban growth. These newest arrivals have thus but assumed the role formerly played by European immigrants.

In the past, New York benefited greatly from the presence of such laborers; but the city and the immigrants paid the cost in debilitating social disorders. Recovery from those disorders came from the capacity to expand and from the freedom with which the newcomers and their children could rise to the opportunities created by the expansion.

The Negroes and the Puerto Ricans have followed the general outline of the experience of earlier immigrants. These latest arrivals diverged from that earlier experience because color prejudice and the social and economic conditions they encountered impeded their freedom of movement, both in space and in social and economic status. That divergence in experience need not be more than temporary, however.

The available evidence sustains the following more concrete conclusions.

1. A pool of potential emigrants will persist in both Puerto Rico and in the South, but it will be drawn upon only to the extent that

opportunities for unskilled labor in New York exist. Both groups will, in any case, however, increase in numbers through internal growth.

2. The genuine problems of social disorder in which Negroes and Puerto Ricans are involved can best be solved through the development of communal institutions, under responsible leadership that will give order and purpose to their lives.

3. The reduction of prejudice and the expansion of opportunities are essential to such development.

4. Such development will not come primarily through the general dispersal of these people in the whole population. Although some individuals, given the freedom to do so, will prefer to scatter in many different districts, the great majority of Negroes and Puerto Ricans, like the other ethnic groups, will continue to live in cohesive settlements. They will be accommodated through the evolution, in the suburbs and in the central city, of numerous neighborhoods at various income levels to which clusters of them will be voluntarily drawn by common interests and tastes.

5. The Negroes and Puerto Ricans are likely to continue, as they have in the past, to depend more on governmental services for education and welfare than did earlier immigrants.

Ultimately the future will be shaped by the men and women who will live through it. But the experience of the past offers a solid foundation for the belief that the newest immigrants to a great cosmopolitan city will come to play as useful a role in it as any of their predecessors. They themselves need only show the will and energy, and their neighbors the tolerance, to make it possible.

ACKNOWLEDGMENTS

APPENDIX

TABLES

ENDNOTES

INDEX

Acknowledgments

In the course of my work upon this monograph I have become indebted for aid to many individuals and groups. Clifford L. Alexander, Jr., proved an ingenious and imaginative assistant and was particularly helpful in developing the material on housing.

For many stimulating suggestions and comments, I am indebted to the scholars who worked on other phases of this study, particularly to its director, Raymond Vernon, and to Edward S. Mason and Edgar M. Hoover. Martin Segal, Max Hall, Milton Abelson, Roy Helfgott, and Robert Wood were also helpful.

Professor Davis McEntire was good enough to let me see the preliminary report of Commission on Race and Housing of which he is research director.

For taking the time to supply helpful information through interviews, I am very grateful to Clarence Senior, Chief, and to Joseph Monserrat, Director, of the New York City Office of Puerto Rican Department of Labor, Migration Division; to Jacques E. Willmore, Housing Secretary of the Westchester Urban League; to Joseph Davis, Executive Vice-President, Carver Savings and Loan Association, and to Richard Brennan, President of the Brevoort Savings Bank.

Other assistance for which I am grateful came from Henry Cohen and Marvin Roth of the New York City Administrator's Office; Blanche Bernstein, Director of Research, Community Council of Greater New York; Daniel S. Anthony, Newark Commission on Group Relations; Aaron Antonovsky, Director of Research, and Eunice and George Grieg of the staff of the New York State Commission Against Discrimination; Daniel Creamer of the National Industrial Conference Board; Britton Harris of the University of Pennsylvania; Theresa Wolfson of Brooklyn College; E. A. Loughran of the U. S. Immigration and Naturalization Service; Herbert E. Klarman, Hospital Council of Greater New York; and H. Daniel Carpenter of Hudson Guild Neighborhood House.

I profited also from the opportunity to discuss the problems of this work with scholars from various disciplines at three conferences, at the Merrill Center for Economics in June 1957; with the Interagency Research Committee of the Community Council of New York City in November 1957, and with a group convened by the Study in August 1958. For the contents of the book, however, I am of course solely responsible.

As so often in the past, I am indebted to Mary Flug Handlin for devoted collaboration. In the preparation of the manuscript, I profited from the efficiency and the patience of Patricia Will, Dorothy Summers, and Pauline Bender.

Oscar Handlin

Cambridge, Massachusetts
May 15, 1959

Appendix

Motives for Negro Migration
to the Suburbs

This data is based on a survey of former tenants of Riverton, a privately owned development in Harlem, built under the Redevelopment Companies Act by the Metropolitan Life Insurance Company. When opened in 1947 it provided three- or four-room apartments for 1,232 families. An examination was made of all families who had moved out of the development in the last five full years, 1952–1956. From this number those who had moved at the request of management were eliminated as well as those who had moved out of the 22 counties included in the New York Metropolitan Region Study. Other names were deleted whenever information was available that the move had occurred because of death in the family, separation, or divorce. Finally, the white families were removed. This left a final sample group of 147 families. They were all Negro and had all moved presumably at their own volition. A letter and accompanying questionnaire were then mailed to the head of each of the 147 households.* Of these, four could not be located through the mail.

Of the final group of 143 who had received the inquiry, 82 returned their questionnaires. This was a response of approximately 60 per cent. There were ten questions where generally a check was all that was required. Some respondents, however, added comments to clarify or expand their answers. Of the 82 respondents, 36 lived within the five boroughs but in such border areas as the upper Bronx or St. Albans, Queens. The remainder (46) lived outside of New

* See below, pp. 127–131 ff.

York City but within the 22-county area specified in the New York Metropolitan Region Study.

The average income of the group could not be ascertained with exactness. A reasonable approximation would seem to be $7,500 per family-unit moving, based upon: the income reported by the tenants when they originally moved in; the general rise in average income during the period of residency; and the probable improvement in salary which resulted from employment changes. More striking was the fact that the educational attainments of the group were unusual. Fully half of them were college graduates; and about 30 per cent had graduate degrees. They were therefore among the most mobile of Negroes. The final totals of answers to the questionnaire are given below.

The initial question concerned itself with the social make-up of the respondents' new neighborhood, as defined by the respondent himself.

It seemed too difficult and, perhaps, unnecessary to attempt to communicate a more precise definition through the questionnaire. The response was as follows: predominantly white, 25; approximately 50 per cent Negro, 33; predominantly Negro, 24.

The second question asked whether any prejudice had been encountered in the search for a suburban dwelling. Forty answered yes; forty-two, no. Of the forty who had actually experienced prejudice in their search for a home, eleven lived in predominantly white neighborhoods. Twenty lived in areas which were approximately 50 per cent Negro and nine in predominantly Negro areas.

The third question was directed at those who had answered the second in the affirmative, in the hope of locating the source of the prejudice shown. One or more possible responses were suggested; and many answers revealed that the prejudice encountered emanated from more than one source. Significantly, 85 per cent of those who had encountered prejudice in their search for a dwelling pointed to real estate brokers as the source of their discomfort. The owners of the property involved and the neighbors showed far less hostility.

To the fourth question, "Have you observed prejudice on the part of your present neighbors?", fifteen answered "yes" and sixty-seven "no." Of the fifteen who responded "yes," six voluntarily added comments, such as: "only a few," "only one, and he has found out through my home that we keep our property just as well as he does," "a mild sort—easy to take (withdrawn)." Of the fifteen who had found prejudice on the part of their present neighbors nine were in predominantly white neighborhoods, one in a mixed neighborhood, and five in predominantly Negro neighborhoods.

Question 5 inquired into the information that led to the respondent's purchase. The numerical breakdown of answers was as follows: newspaper listings? 23; friends who lived in the suburbs? 33; a real estate broker? 35; an organizational listing 1.*

An analysis of these answers by the racial composition of the neighborhoods to which respondents moved showed somewhat surprisingly that real estate brokers were more likely to be useful in mixed or white, than in colored, areas.

	Predominantly White	Approx. 50% White	Predominantly Negro
Newspaper listings	3	6	8
Friends who live in the suburbs	7	7	9
A real estate broker	11	10	4
An organizational listing	0	0	1
Both newspaper listings and friends in the suburbs	1	1	1
Friends in the suburbs and a real estate broker	2	5	0
Newspaper listings and a real estate broker	0	3	0

The answers to question 6, which gave the reasons for the move from the central city, showed the primacy of middle-class motives.

* The Urban League and the Intergroup Relations Commission are two of the groups which have published listings where Negroes are by law able to acquire houses or apartments without fear of prejudice.

	No.
wished to live nearer to place of employment	2
wanted to own own home	72
felt restricted by apartment living	47
felt children would be afforded better educational opportunity	40 *
wanted to reside in an integrated community	20

Of the forty who felt their children would have better educational opportunities in their new neighborhoods, fifteen moved to predominantly white areas, eighteen to areas which are 50 per cent white, and the remaining seven to communities which are predominantly Negro. Twenty listed a desire to reside in an integrated neighborhood as one of their reasons for moving from the central city. None of the respondents listed this as the sole reason for departure, however. Of the twenty, eight live in areas which are predominantly white, nine in 50 per cent areas, and three in communities predominantly Negro in racial composition.

Question 7 was intended to indicate how respondents were using their new homes, on the presumption that subdivision often tends to deteriorate a structure more rapidly than normal wear and tear. Seventy-two had no lodgers, and, of the ten that did, one had a white lodger, seven had Negro lodgers, and two had both white and Negro lodgers.

The responses to question 8 revealed that almost all still maintained some ties to the neighborhoods they had left: close ties, 24; occasional visits, 61; none, 2.† Those ties, the answers to question 9 showed, were sustained through: church affiliations, 17; political clubs or organizations, 6; fraternal or social organizations, 27; civic

* Not all of the respondents had children so that 40 represents a higher percentage than would appear on surface examination. It is impossible to ascertain the exact percentage of respondents with children. Approximately 65 per cent of those who were sent questionnaires had children. Some few also moved because a child was on the way.

† The total is five over the total number of respondents included. The extras indicated that one member of the family maintained close ties while the other only made occasional visits to his old neighborhood.

organizations, 7; friends, 47; business or employment, 7; army, 1. Four of the twenty-four who maintained close ties lived in predominantly white communities; fifteen in areas approximately 50 per cent white, and five in predominantly Negro neighborhoods. Those close ties were distributed as follows:

Church affiliations	1
Fraternal or social organizations	2
Friends	6
Church affiliations and fraternal or social organizations	5
Fraternal or social organizations and friends	1
Church affiliations and friends	3
Political clubs or organizations and fraternal or social organizations	1
Political clubs or organizations and civic organizations	1
Fraternal, social, and civic organizations	1
Fraternal or social organizations and the Army	1
Employment	1
Civic organizations and friends	1

Question 10 ascertained the level of educational attainment of respondents. The breakdown was as follows:

Less than high school	3
High school	31
High school and some college training	7
Completed college	16
Completed graduate school	25
4 lawyers	
5 doctors	
16 other (PhD's; M.A.'s; M.B.A.'s; etc.)	

A comparison of the level of educational achievement and the racial composition of neighborhoods revealed the following:

	Less than High School	High School	High School plus	College	Grad. degree
Predominantly white	1	5	0	6	13
50% White	1	16	2	4	10
Predominantly Negro	1	10	5	6	2

Of the forty respondents who encountered prejudice in their search for a surburban dwelling, fourteen were high school graduates, two had some college training, seven had completed college, and seventeen held a graduate degree.

Of the fifteen persons who had noticed prejudice on the part of their present neighbors, three were high school graduates, one had some college training, four were college graduates, and seven had received a graduate degree. Of the six who modified their answers with a comment, one was a high school graduate, two were college graduates, and three held graduate degrees.

Responses to the Questionnaire

Directions: Please place an *x* in the appropriate blank. If more than one answer applies to your situation please mark all the applicable blanks.

* * * * * * * * *

1. Is your present neighborhood:
   25 predominantly white?
   33 approximately 50% white?
   24 predominantly Negro?

2. Did you encounter any prejudice in your search for a suburban dwelling?
   40 YES
   42 NO

3. Was this prejudice shown by:
   34 real estate brokers?
   17 owners of property you inspected?
   11 others. Specify: (generally neighbors)

4. Have you observed prejudice on the part of your present neighbors?
   15 Yes (6 comments)
   67 No (5 comments)

5. What information led you to your purchase:
   23 newspaper listings?
   33 friends who live in the suburbs?
   35 a real estate broker?
   1 an organizational listing?

6. Did you move from the central city for one or more of the following reasons:
    2 you wished to live nearer your place of employment?
    72 you wanted to own your own home?
    47 you felt restricted space-wise by apartment living?
    40 you felt your children would be afforded better educational opportunity in your present neighborhood?
    20 you wanted to reside in an integrated community?

7. Do you have lodgers and if so are they:
    1 white?
    7 Negro?
    2 both white and Negro?
    72 no lodgers

8. Although you now reside in the suburbs do you maintain any ties with your former neighborhood?
    24 close ties?
    62 occasional visits?
    2 none?

9. Are these ties through:
    17 church affiliations?
    6 political clubs or organizations?
    27 fraternal or social organizations?
    7 civic organizations?
    others. Specify: friends 47; business employment 7; army 1

10. Have you completed:
    31 High School? less than high school 3; high school plus 7
    16 College?
    25 Graduate school (please write in graduate degrees received)?
    (4 lawyers; 5 doctors; 16 others)

Table 1   Estimated Population of New York, 1656–1786

Year	White	Negro	Total
1656	—	—	1,000
1664	—	—	1,500
1698	4,237	700	4,937
1703	3,806	630	4,436
1712	—	—	5,840
1723	5,886	1,362	7,248
1731	7,045	1,577	8,622
1746	9,273	2,444	11,717
1756	10,768	2,278	13,046
1771	18,726	3,137	21,863
1786	21,507	2,103	23,610

Source: E. B. Greene and V. D. Harrington, *American Population Before the Federal Census of 1790* (New York: 1932), 94–104.

Table 2   Population of New York City,[a] 1790–1820

1790	33,131
1800	60,489
1810	96,373
1820	112,706

[a] As then constituted, not the whole of Manhattan Island.

Source: J. D. B. DeBow, *Statistical View of the United States* (Washington, 1852), 192.

Table 3   Population of New York City, 1820–1870

Year	Manhattan Island	Brooklyn [a]
1820	123,706	11,187
1830	197,112	20,535
1840	312,710	47,613
1850	515,547	138,882
1860	813,669	279,122
1870	942,292	419,921

[a] The area included in the Borough of Brooklyn as constituted under the act of consolidation of 1898.

Source: Fifteenth Census, *Population,* I, 18, 19.

Table 4 Negro Population, Slave and Free,
New York State, 1790–1860

Year	Slave	Free
1790	21,193	4,682
1800	20,903	10,417
1810	15,017	25,333
1820	10,088	29,279
1830	75	44,870
1840	4	50,027
1850	0	49,069
1860	0	49,005

Source: Bureau of the Census, *Negro Population, 1790–1915* (Washington, 1918), 57.

Table 5 Colored Population of New York City, 1860

Place of Birth	Number
New York State	7,863
New Jersey	1,166
Delaware, Pennsylvania	795
New England	533
Virginia, Maryland	1,331
Other slave states	324
Other, United States	62
West Indies	207
Others	288
Total	12,569

Source: *Eighth Census.*

Table 6 White Population of New York City, 1860

Birthplace	Number
New York	371,166
New Jersey, Pennsylvania	17,129
New England	20,252
Other U.S.	9,245
Germany [a]	119,984
Ireland	203,740
Scotland	9,208
England	27,082
France	8,074
Others	15,422
Total	801,302

[a] Includes Austria.

Source: *Eighth Census.*

Table 7 Population of New York City, 1870–1950

Year	Manhattan	Bronx	Brooklyn	Queens	Richmond	Total
1870	942,292	37,393	419,921	45,468	33,029	1,478,103
1880	1,164,673	51,980	599,495	56,559	38,991	1,911,698
1890	1,441,216	88,908	838,547	87,050	51,693	2,507,414
1900	1,850,093	200,507	1,166,582	152,999	67,021	3,437,202
1910	2,331,542	430,980	1,634,351	284,041	85,969	4,766,883
1920	2,284,103	732,016	2,018,356	469,042	116,531	5,620,048
1930	1,867,312	1,265,258	2,560,401	1,079,129	158,346	6,930,446
1940	1,889,924	1,394,711	2,698,285	1,297,634	174,441	7,454,995
1950	1,960,101	1,451,277	2,738,175	1,550,849	191,555	7,891,957

Source: U.S. Fifteenth, Seventeenth Censuses, *Population.*

Table 8 Population of New York City and Vicinity, by Color and Place of Birth, 1910

	Manhattan	Bronx	Brooklyn	Queens	Richmond	Total New York City	Newark	Jersey City
Negro								
New York State	14,309	1,484	8,768	1,805	611	26,977	3,931	1,500
Other states	37,001	2,266	11,182	1,284	469	52,202	5,331	4,278
Other native	485	23	254	7	4	773	66	27
Foreign-born	8,739	344	2,504	102	68	11,757	147	155
Total	60,534	4,117	22,708	3,198	1,152	91,709	9,475	5,960
White								
New York State	991,167	249,388	937,250	184,628	51,885	2,414,318	179,529	129,879
Other states	159,438	27,278	99,849	16,502	8,410	311,477	46,441	53,489
Other native	11,954	1,049	2,032	446	183	15,664	1,117	594
Foreign-born	1,104,019	148,935	571,356	79,115	24,278	1,927,703	110,655	77,697
Total	2,266,578	426,650	1,610,487	280,691	84,756	4,669,162	337,742	261,659
Other colored	4,430	213	1,156	152	61	6,012	252	160
Total	2,331,542	430,980	1,634,351	284,041	85,969	4,766,883	347,469	267,779

Source: *Negro Population*, 74.

Table 9 Commuters Carried Daily by Leading Railroads, 1929

Grand Central Terminal	42,500
Bronx Terminals	8,900
Long Island Railroad	63,000
New Jersey Railroads	144,000
Total	258,400

Source: Regional Plan of New York, *Graphic Regional Plan* (New York, 1929), I, 192ff.

Table 10 Foreign White Stock in New York City, 1940

Nationality	Number
Italian	1,095,369
Russian [a]	926,516
Irish	518,466
German	498,289
Polish [a]	412,543
Austrian [a]	322,586
British	216,663
Scandinavian	126,516
Hungarian [a]	123,188
Rumanian [a]	84,675
Czech	57,624
Greek	53,253
Others	395,892
Total	4,831,580

[a] These include substantial numbers of Jews. The Jewish population of New York City was estimated from other sources at 2,000,000.

Source: Derived from the 5 per cent sample of the 1940 census.

Table 11 Alien Address Reports Received
from New York City, 1958

Nationality	Number of Persons
Germany	34,410
Great Britain and Canada	43,470
Greece	9,572
Italy	63,287
Poland	23,901
U.S.S.R.	19,980
China	9,406
Mexico	1,738
All other	164,779
Total	370,543

Source: Supplied by Immigration and Naturalization Service; figures for
the state are in *I and N Reporter,* July, 1958, p. 14; April, 1959, p. 56.

Table 12 Percentage of Negroes in the Population
of New York State, 1790–1910

Year	Per cent
1790	7.6
1800	5.3
1810	4.2
1820	2.9
1830	2.3
1840	2.1
1850	1.6
1860	1.3
1870	1.2
1880	1.3
1890	1.2
1900	1.4
1910	1.5

Source: *Negro Population,* 51.

Table 13 Native Negro Population

Negroes	1870	1880	1890	1900	1910
Total, born in South	4,548,991	6,124,351	6,908,869	8,216,458	9,109,153
Born in South, living in North and West	149,100	198,029	241,855	349,651	440,534
Per cent	3.3	3.2	3.5	4.3	4.8
Increase over previous decade	—	48,929	43,826	107,796	90,883
Total, born in North and West	319,897	442,357	481,101	570,089	636,890
Born in North and West, living in South	15,583	22,039	23,268	30,397	41,489
Per cent	4.9	5.0	4.8	5.3	6.5
Increase over previous decade	—	6,456	1,229	7,129	11,092
Net gain of North and West	133,517	175,990	118,587	319,254	399,045
Increase over previous decade	—	42,473	—57,403	200,667	79,791

Source: *Negro Population,* 65.

Table 14 Negro Population of Large Municipalites other than New York City in the New York Metropolitan Region, 1910, 1950

Municipalities	1910	1950
Newark	9,475	35,797
Jersey City	5,960	9,882
Montclair	2,485	4,085
Orange	2,479	3,120
East Orange	1,907	4,862
New Rochelle	1,754	3,146
Paterson	1,539	3,932
Elizabeth	1,381	3,529
Bridgeport	1,332	3,397
Princeton	1,148	444
Mt. Vernon	896	3,414
Hempstead	242	1,181

Source: Thirteenth, Seventeenth Censuses of Population.

Table 15 New York State Native Negro Population,
by Nativity, 1910

Birthplace	Number
New England	2,352
Middle Atlantic	55,056
East North Central	1,198
West North Central	478
South Atlantic	57,585
East South Central	2,255
West South Central	654
Mountain	164
Pacific	287
Other, United States	894
Total, United States	120,923
Outlying possessions	417
Total native	121,340

Source: *Negro Population,* 75.

Table 16 Foreign-born Negroes,
United States, 1850–1910

Year	Number
1850	4,067
1860	4,363
1870	9,645
1880	14,017
1890	19,979
1900	20,236
1910	40,339

Source: *Negro Population,* 61.

Table 17 Rate of Increase of Puerto Rico's Population, 1887–1956
(per thousand)

Year	Annual birth rate	Annual death rate	Rate of natural increase
1887–1899 [a]	45.7	31.4	14.3
1899–1910 [a]	40.5	25.3	15.2
1910–1920 [a]	40.4	24.0	16.4
1920–1930 [a]	39.3	22.1	17.2
1930–1935 [a]	39.0	20.1	18.9
1935–1940 [a]	40.2	19.2	21.0
1941–1945 [a]	40.6	15.8	24.8
1946–1950 [a]	40.9	11.6	29.3
1950	38.7	9.9	28.8
1951	37.6	10.0	27.6
1952	35.8	9.2	26.6
1953	34.7	8.1	26.6
1954	35.0	7.6	27.4
1955	35.0	7.2	27.8
1956 (preliminary)	34.1	7.3	26.8

[a] Average

Source: *A Summary in Facts and Figures,* April 1957, p. 3.

Table 18 Population of Puerto Rico, 1860–1956

Year	Number
1860	583,308
1877	731,648
1887	798,565
1899	953,243
1910	1,118,012
1920	1,299,809
1930	1,543,913
1940	1,869,000
1950	2,211,000
1956 [a]	2,276,000

[a] Estimate

Source: From census and *A Summary in Facts and Figures,* April, 1957, p. 2.

Table 19 Net Puerto Rican Migration
to the Continental United States

Year	Number
1909–1930 [a]	1,986
1931–1940 [a]	904
1941–1950 [a]	18,794
1946	39,911
1947	24,551
1948	32,775
1949	25,698
1950	34,703
1951	52,899
1952	59,103
1953	69,124
1954	21,531
1955	45,464
1956	52,315

[a] Annual average

Source: *A Summary in Facts and Figures,* April, 1957, p. 15.

Table 20 Puerto Rican Population of Continental United States,
1940–1956 [a]

Date	Total	Puerto Rican birth	Puerto Rican parentage
April 1940	[b]	69,967	[b]
April 1950	301,375	226,110	75,265
Dec. 31, 1950	337,000	254,000	83,000
Dec. 31, 1951	400,000	306,000	94,000
Dec. 31, 1952	472,000	364,000	108,000
Dec. 31, 1953	557,000	432,000	125,000
Dec. 31, 1954	597,000	452,000	145,000
Dec. 31, 1955	662,000	496,000	166,000
Dec. 31, 1956	736,000	547,000	189,000

[a] Data for April 1940 and April 1950 from U.S. censuses. Subsequent data estimated on basis of net out-migration from Puerto Rico, Puerto Rican birth rates in New York City, and death rates of Puerto Rican-born persons in New York City (for estimates of population of Puerto Rican parentage).

[b] Not available

Source: *A Summary in Facts and Figures;* A. J. Jaffe, ed., *Puerto Rican Population of New York City* (New York, 1954), 4.

Table 21 Puerto Rican Migration to New York City, 1950–1956

Year	Estimated migration to New York City	Per cent of total migration
1950	29,500	85
1951	42,300	80
1952	45,500	77
1953	51,800	75
1954	16,100	75
1955	31,800	70
1956	34,000	65

Source: *A Summary in Facts and Figures,* April, 1957, p. 16.

Table 22 Puerto Rican Population of New York City, 1940–1956

Date [a]	Total	Puerto Rican Birth	Puerto Rican Parentage
April 1940	[b]	61,463	[b]
April 1950	245,880	187,420	58,460
Dec. 31, 1950	276,000	211,000	65,000
Dec. 31, 1951	328,000	253,000	75,000
Dec. 31, 1952	383,000	297,000	86,000
Dec. 31, 1953	448,000	348,000	100,000
Dec. 31, 1954	479,000	363,000	116,000
Dec. 31, 1955	527,000	394,000	133,000
Dec. 31, 1956	577,000 [c]	426,000	151,000

[a] Data for April 1940 and April 1950 from U.S. censuses. Subsequent data estimated on basis of out-migration from Puerto Rico, estimated per cent of migrants settling in New York City, Puerto Rican birth rates in the city, death rates of Puerto Rican-born persons in the city (for estimates of population of Puerto Rican birth), and general death rates (for population of Puerto Rican parentage).

[b] Not available

[c] Estimated at 550,000 by New York City Department of City Planning, allowing for estimated out-migration from the city to other parts of the United States, all estimates assumed subject to about 10 per cent error.

Source: *A Summary in Facts and Figures;* Jaffe, *Puerto Rican Population,* 6.

Table 23   Negroes in the United States, Percentage Increase
in Preceding Decade, 1800–1910

Year	All Classes	Negro	White
1800	35.1	32.3	35.8
1810	36.4	37.5	36.1
1820	33.1	28.6	34.2
1830	33.5	31.4	33.9
1840	32.7	23.4	34.7
1850	35.9	26.6	37.7
1860	35.6	22.1	37.7
1870	22.6	9.9	24.8
1880	30.1	34.9	29.2
1890	25.5	13.8	27.0
1900	20.7	18.0	21.2
1910	21.0	11.2	22.3

Source: *Negro Population*, 25.

Table 24   Percentage of Public Elementary and High School
Students, by Ethnic Groups, 1957

Borough	Negro	Puerto Rican	Others
Richmond	5.8	1.2	93.0
Queens	10.7	1.4	87.9
Manhattan	34.5	32.0	33.5
Bronx	15.3	19.3	65.4
Brooklyn	17.3	10.7	72.0
Total	18.3	14.0	67.7
Actual number of students	132,402	101,671	491,161

Source: Figures obtained from Report on Integration No. 1, by the Superintendent of Schools.

Table 25 Distribution of Puerto Rican and Foreign-born Pupils, by Borough and Total, October 31, 1956

Borough	Total register	Puerto Rican	Foreign-born	Total Puerto Rican and foreign-born	Per cent Puerto Rican and foreign-born
Manhattan	174,271	48,952	7,128	56,080	32.2
Bronx	173,683	30,417	4,825	35,242	20.3
Brooklyn	336,795	30,078	8,621	38,699	11.5
Queens	210,299	2,846	6,676	9,522	4.5
Richmond	28,460	448	391	839	3.0
Special schools	4,490	1,146	72	1,218	27.1
City-wide total	927,998	113,887	27,713	141,600	15.3

Source: *The Puerto Rican Study* (New York, 1958), 171.

Table 26 Comparison of Census Summaries of 1955 and 1956, Puerto Ricans and Foreign-born, New York City Public Schools

	1955	1956	Increase
Number of pupils			
Puerto Rican	102,554	113,887	11,333
Foreign-born	23,564	27,713	4,149
Total	126,118	141,600	15,482
Total register	898,587	927,998	29,411
Per cent of total register			
Puerto Rican	11.4	12.3	0.9
Foreign-born	2.6	3.0	0.4
Total	14.0	15.3	1.3

Source: *The Puerto Rican Study,* 170.

Table 27 Assembly Districts in New York City, 1910,
with More than 5 Per Cent Negroes

Borough	District	Number of Negroes	Percentage of total
Manhattan		60,534	2.6
Manhattan	13	9,273	17.7
Manhattan	21	10,921	14.9
Manhattan	9	5,361	9.8
Manhattan	30	7,556	8.2
Manhattan	27	3,548	6.4
Brooklyn		22,708	1.4
Brooklyn	1	3,110	6.2
Bronx		4,117	1.0
Queens		3,198	1.1
Richmond		1,152	1.3
Total, city		91,709	1.9

Source: Derived from *Negro Population,* 106, 107.

Table 28 New Jersey Wards with More
than 5 Per Cent Negroes, 1910

City	Ward	Number of Negroes	Per cent of total population
Newark	2	1,577	11.5
Newark	4	1,037	7.5
Newark	7	1,441	6.4
Jersey City	8	1,677	5.4
Jersey City	6	928	5.3
Total, Newark		9,475	2.7
Total, Jersey City		5,960	2.2

Source: Derived from material in *Negro Population,* 106.

Table 29 Percentage of Public Housing in New York City
Occupied by Negroes

Date	Per cent
December 1951	27.97
December 1956	38.5
March 1957	38.8

Source: See Table 30.

Table 30 Occupants of Public Housing, by Ethnic Groups,
March 1957

			City classification				
	Federal	State	Part I	Part II	Part III	Part IV	Total
Maximum family income for eligibility	$4,000	$5,964	$4,000	$5,400	$5,400	$6,900	—
Units Available	34,428	31,184	1,552	4,696	16,401	2,144	90,405
Units Occupied	34,378	31,147	1,549	4,696	16,389	2,144	90,298
White (per cent)	41.1	28.4	52.7	64.7	79.5	92.7	46.3
Negro (per cent)	41.7	50.6	22.6	31.5	18.0	6.5	38.8
Puerto Rican (per cent)	16.9	20.5	24.2	3.5	2.4	0.7	13.4

Source: Data obtained from New York City Housing Authority.

Table 31 Puerto Rican Population, by Boroughs, 1956

Area	Total population	Puerto Rican population	Per cent of total
New York City [a]	8,075,000	577,000	7.1
Manhattan [b]	1,910,000	240,000	12.6
Bronx [b]	1,500,000	130,000	8.7
Brooklyn [b]	2,710,000	105,000	3.9
Queens [b]	1,720,000	10,000	0.6
Richmond [b]	210,000	[c]	[c]

[a] Data for December 31, 1956.
[b] Data for December 31, 1954, latest available estimate.
[c] Less than 2,500; less than 1.2 per cent.

Source: *A Summary in Facts and Figures,* 13.

NOTES

CHAPTER 1: INTRODUCTION

1. See, for example, Harry L. Shapiro, "Immigration and Cultural Adjustment," Community Council of Greater New York, *Our Changing Community* (New York, 1957), 10.

CHAPTER 2: THE HISTORICAL BACKGROUND, 1620–1928

1. See, in general, E. L. Raesly, *Portrait of New Netherland* (New York, 1945); J. G. Wilson, *Memorial History of the City of New York* (New York, 1892), I, 152ff.

2. Table 1; Carl Bridenbaugh, *Cities in the Wilderness* (New York, 1938) and *Cities in Revolt* (New York, 1955); Wilson, *Memorial History*, I, 307ff., 341ff., II, 195, 449; Hyman B. Grinstein, *Rise of the Jewish Community of New York 1654–1860* (Philadelphia, 1945), 21ff.; James W. Johnson, *Black Manhattan* (New York, 1930), 5ff.

3. Robert A. East, *Business Enterprise in the American Revolutionary Era* (New York, 1938), 121ff., 180ff., 235ff.; Oscar T. Barck, *New York City during the War for Independence* (New York, 1931), 120ff.; Sidney I. Pomerantz, *New York an American City 1783–1803* (New York, 1938), 147ff.

4. Table 2; *Fourth Census*, 15; Pomerantz, *New York*, 199ff.; Wilson, *Memorial History*, III, 1ff.

5. William J. Bromwell, *History of Immigration to the United States* (New York, 1856), 15ff.; Friedrich Kapp, *Immigration and the Commissioners of Emigration of the State of New York* (New York, 1870), 7ff.

6. Pomerantz, *New York*, 203ff., 220ff.

7. Society for the Prevention of Pauperism in the City of New York, *Second Annual Report of the Managers* (New York, 1820), 18ff.

8. See maps in Thomas Adams, *et al., Building of the City. Regional Plan*, II (New York, 1931), 38, 40, 50.

9. John H. Griscom, *Sanitary Condition of the Laboring Population of New York* (New York, 1845), 14; Kate H. Claghorn, "The Foreign Immigrant in New York City," United States Industrial Commission, *Reports on Immigration* (Washington, 1901), XV, 451.

10. On the general economic development of the city in this period, see R. G. Albion, *Rise of New York Port 1815–1860* (New York, 1939); Wilson, *Memorial History*, III, 334ff., 413ff.

11. Table 3.

12. Table 6; also R. G. Albion, "Yankee Domination of New York Port, 1820–1865," *New England Quarterly*, V (1932), 665ff.

13. DeBow, *Statistical View,* 192; Tables 4, 5; Johnson, *Black Manhattan,* 13ff.

14. Charles H. Wesley, *Negro Labor in the United States 1850–1925* (New York, 1927), 37–38; Johnson, *Black Manhattan,* 20ff.; George E. Haynes, *Negro at Work in New York City* (New York, 1912), 67, 96ff.; below, p. 46.

15. For a general account of the immigrants of this period, see Robert Ernst, *Immigrant Life in New York City, 1825–1863* (New York, 1949); and Kate H. Claghorn, "The Foreign Immigrant in New York City," United States Industrial Commission, *Reports on Immigration* (Washington, 1901), XV, 449ff.

16. On the general background, see Marcus L. Hansen, *The Atlantic Migration* (Cambridge, 1940); Oscar Handlin, *The Uprooted* (Boston, 1951).

17. Claghorn, "Foreign Immigrant," 462.

18. Table 6; *Ninth Census,* I, 386.

19. Ernst, *Immigrant Life,* 164.

20. Ernst, *Immigrant Life,* 61ff.; John R. Commons, "Immigration and Its Economic Effects," U.S. Industrial Commission, *Reports on Immigration* (Washington, 1901), XV, 324. For a further discussion of social mobility, see below, p. 46.

21. A map showing population density as of 1860 was prepared by the Tenement House Commission of 1894 and is reproduced in *Harper's Weekly,* January 19, 1895, p. 62. See also the successive maps, published by M. Dripps, and John M. Atwood, *Map of the City of New York* (New York, 1855); Harry J. Carman, *Street Surface Railway Franchises of New York City* (New York, 1919), 146.

22. Wilson, *Memorial History,* II, 188ff.

23. On housing in this period, see Claghorn, "Foreign Immigrant," 452ff.; Ernst, *Immigrant Life,* 48ff.; John H. Griscom, *Sanitary Condition of the Laboring Population of New York* (New York, 1845).

24. See Anna A. Chapin, *Greenwich Village* (New York, 1917), 35ff., 103ff.; Caroline F. Ware, *Greenwich Village 1920–1930* (Boston, 1935), 9ff.; Carman, *Street Railway Franchises,* 39ff.

25. See, for example, Charles F. Briggs, *The Trippings of Tom Pepper* (New York, 1847), I, 110; also Claghorn, "Foreign Immigrant," 458.

26. Ernst, *Immigrant Life,* 37ff.; Claghorn, "Foreign Immigrant," 457.

27. Materials for a comparison, based on Maryland and Massachusetts data, will be found in Paul H. Jacobson, "Estimate of the Expectation of Life in the United States in 1850," *Milbank Memorial Fund Quarterly,* XXXV (1957), 197ff. See also John H. Griscom, *Sanitary Legislation* (New York, 1861), 8–10, 15; Claghorn, "Foreign Immigrant," 450ff., 453.

28. *Report of a Committee Appointed by the Society for the Prevention of Pauperism in the City of New York on the Expediency of Erecting an Institution for the Reformation of Juvenile Delinquents* (New York, 1824), 6. In general, see also Ernst, *Immigrant Life,* 53ff.

29. Ernst, *Immigrant Life,* 58.

30. Claghorn, "Foreign Immigrant," 460. See also Charles F. Briggs, *Bankrupt Stories. The Haunted Merchant* (New York, 1843), 28ff.

31. Claghorn, "Foreign Immigrant," 459.

32. Ernst, *Immigrant Life,* 102ff.

33. Wesley, *Negro Labor,* 100ff.; Ernst, *Immigrant Life,* 174ff.; Wilson, *Memorial History,* III, 502ff.

34. See Louis D. Scisco, *Political Nativism in New York State* (New York, 1901).

35. Ernst, *Immigrant Life,* 122ff., 134ff.; Claghorn, "Foreign Immigrant," 455.

36. Carl Wittke, *Refugees of Revolution* (Philadelphia, 1952), 161ff., 203ff., 270; Henry J. Browne, "The Archdiocese of New York a Century Ago," United States Catholic Historical Society, *Historical Records and Studies,* XXXIX (1952), 129ff.

37. Ernst, *Immigrant Life,* 132ff.

38. Ernst, *Immigrant Life,* 108, 112ff.

39. On the spread of the city and consolidation see Allan Nevins and John A. Krout, *The Greater City* (New York, 1948); Harold C. Syrett, *City of Brooklyn 1865–1898* (New York, 1944), 258ff.

40. A. C. Flick, ed., *History of the State of New York* (New York, 1935–37), VIII, 129ff., 192ff.; X, 3ff., 173ff.

41. Table 7.

42. In general, on the period 1871–1900 see Claghorn, "Foreign Immigrant," 465ff. See also below, p. 46.

43. United States Industrial Commission, *Reports on Immigration* (Washington, 1901), XV, 280; Table 8.

44. See, in general, Works Progress Administration, *The Italians of New York* (New York, 1938); Lawrence F. Pisani, *The Italian in America* (New York, 1957); John H. Mariano, *Second Generation of Italians in New York City* (Boston, [1921]), 12ff.; *Charities,* XII (1904), 443ff.

45. Oscar Handlin, *Adventure in Freedom* (New York, 1954), 80ff.; Moses Rischin, "Jewish Life and Labor in New York City 1870–1914" (Harvard University Ph.D. thesis, 1957).

46. See Kate H. Claghorn, "Agricultural Distribution of Immigrants," United States Industrial Commission, *Reports on Immigration* (Washington, 1901), 492ff.

47. United States Industrial Commission, *Reports on Immigration,* XV, x.

48. Commons, "Immigration and Its Economic Effects," 305. See also, in general, Brinley Thomas, *Migration and Economic Growth* (Cambridge, 1954), 83ff.; Harry Jerome, *Migration and Business Cycles* (New York, 1926).

49. Commons, "Immigration and Its Economic Effects," 298, 385; Mariano, *Second Generation Italians,* 32ff.; Jane E. Robbins, "Bohemian Women in New York," *Charities,* XIII (1904), 194ff.

50. See U.S. Industrial Commission, *Reports on Immigration*, XV, xxivff., xxxii; Commons, "Immigration and Its Economic Effects," 316ff., 345, 368. There are interesting pictures in *Harper's Weekly*, February 9, 1895, p. 136.

51. Commons, "Immigration and Its Economic Effects," 293ff., 318, 325.

52. U.S. Industrial Commission, *Reports on Immigration*, XV, 442ff.

53. See Claghorn, "Foreign Immigrant," 473.

54. U.S. Industrial Commission, *Reports on Immigration*, XV, 430ff.; Edwin Fenton, "Immigrants and Unions. A Case Study: Italians and American Labor, 1870–1920" (Harvard University Ph.D. thesis, 1958).

55. Commons, "Immigration and Its Economic Effects," 369.

56. Ware, *Greenwich Village*, 67ff.; Oscar Handlin, *Al Smith and His America* (Boston, 1958), 18ff.

57. See, for example, Eddie Cantor, *My Life Is in Your Hands* (New York, 1928); Michael Pupin, *From Immigrant to Inventor* (New York, 1923).

58. Ware, *Greenwich Village*, 56ff., 71, 273. There is a good deal of material relevant to this point in 81 Congress, [Kefauver] Senate Special Committee to Investigate Organized Crime in Interstate Commerce, *Hearings*, Part 7.

59. See, on the general problem, Thomas, *Migration and Economic Growth*, 141ff.; Oscar Handlin, "Ethnic Factors in Social Mobility," *Explorations in Entrepreneurial History* (1956).

60. For data on the percentage of various groups in the high schools, see Mariano, *Second Generation Italians*, 62, 63. See also Claghorn, "Foreign Immigrant," 477; Ware, *Greenwich Village*, 68; Handlin, *Al Smith*, 146ff.

61. For a discussion of vocational ambitions, see Mariano, *Second Generation Italians*, 35, 36; Leonard Covello, *The Heart Is the Teacher* (New York, 1958), 29, 128ff. See also Claghorn, "Foreign Immigrant," 475; Ware, *Greenwich Village*, 337ff.

62. There is an informative discussion, together with helpful maps, in Claghorn, "Foreign Immigrant," 470ff. These may be compared with the maps for 1860, 1890, and 1894 prepared for the Tenement House Commission and reproduced in *Harper's Weekly*, January 19, 1895, pp. 60–62. See also G. B. L. Arner, "Land Values in New York City," *Quarterly Journal of Economics*, XXXVI (1922), 545.

63. Ware, *Greenwich Village*, 82ff.; Mariano, *Second Generation Italians*, 27.

64. Claghorn, "Foreign Immigrant," 476.

65. Ware, *Greenwich Village*, 293ff., 467.

66. Ware, *Greenwich Village*, 82ff.

67. *Map Showing the Condition of Buildings in New York City from the Battery to 135th Street* (Survey of February, 1881, otherwise unidentified, HCL, Map 3585.21.2).

68. The settlement of the west side in the last two decades of the century is described in *Harper's Weekly*, July 25, 1896, pp. 730ff.

69. Map, *Harper's Weekly*, August 1, 1896, p. 755; Richard Barry, "How People Come and Go in New York (illus.)," *ibid.*, February 26, 1898, pp.

204ff.; New York Chapter, American Institute of Architects, Committee on Housing, *Riverside, a Study of Housing on the West Side of Manhattan* (New York, 1954), II, 5ff.; Syrett, *Brooklyn*, 17. There is a political history of the surface lines in Carman, *Street Railway Franchises*, 108ff., 143ff., 175. Passenger figures are given *ibid.*, 145. See also W. C. Clark, "Some Considerations Affecting the Long-Term Trend of the Building Industry," *Review of Economic Statistics*, VIII (1926), 47ff.

70. Caroline F. Ware, *Greenwich Village 1920–1930* (Boston, 1935), 17ff.; Thomas J. Jones, *The Sociology of a New York City Block* (New York, 1904), 21.

71. Table 9; Harry A. Gordon, *Subway Nickels* (New York, 1925), 11ff., 23.

72. Richard O'Connor, *Hell's Kitchen* (Philadelphia, 1958), 37ff.

73. See Ware, *Greenwich Village*, 193ff.

74. Ware, *Greenwich Village*, 11ff.; Syrett, *Brooklyn*, 18, 19. For foreigners in New Jersey, see Joseph Atkinson, *History of Newark* (Newark, 1878), 194ff.

75. See W. Bengough, "The Mulberry Bend Italian Colony," *Harper's Weekly*, June 29, 1895, 607; Mariano, *Second Generation Italians*, 51ff.

76. W. Bengough, "The Russo-Jewish Colony," *Harper's Weekly*, August 3, 1895, XXXIX, 725, 726; Leo Grebler, *Housing Market Behavior in a Declining Area. Long-term Changes in Inventory and Utilization of Housing on New York's Lower East Side* (New York, 1952), 10ff.

77. W. Bengough, "The Syrian Colony," *Harper's Weekly*, August 3, 1895, XXXIX, 746; Mary B. Sayles, "Housing and Social Conditions in a Slavic Neighborhood," *Charities*, XIII (1904), 257ff.; Federal Writers' Project, *New York City Guide* (New York, 1939), 104ff.; Louis H. Pink, "Magyar in New York," *Charities*, XIII, 262ff.; Grebler, *Housing Market Behavior*, 146ff.

78. Grebler, *Housing Market Behavior*, 124, 135ff., 142ff.

79. Ware, *Greenwich Village*, 11ff.; Mariano, *Second Generation Italians*, 19ff.; Jones, *Sociology of a City Block*, 22; Covello, *The Heart Is the Teacher*, 21ff., 175ff.; Grebler, *Housing Market Behavior*, 19, 139ff.

80. Maps in Thomas Adams, *et al.*, *Building of the City. Regional Plan*, II (New York, 1931), 401; Ware, *Greenwich Village*, 24ff.; Grebler, *Housing Market Behavior*, 15ff., 107, 148ff.; below, p. 65.

81. Ware, *Greenwich Village*, 29; Grebler, *Housing Market Behavior*, 110–122.

82. There is an account of tenement development, with good illustrations and plans, in *Harper's Weekly*, January 12, 1895, p. 42, and June 22, 1895, pp. 586, 587. See also, Claghorn, "Foreign Immigrant," 484–491; Adams, *Building of City*, 57.

83. U.S. Industrial Commission, *Reports on Immigration*, XV, 442ff.

84. Claghorn, "Foreign Immigrant," 478ff., 491.

85. O'Connor, *Hell's Kitchen*, 55ff., 117ff.

86. On Irish-Italian differences in intemperance, dependency, and gambling, see Ware, *Greenwich Village*, 136, 388ff.; Jones, *Sociology of a City*

Block, 46. See also Sophia M. Robison, *Can Delinquency Be Measured?* (New York, 1937), 156ff.

87. Ware, *Greenwich Village,* 404ff.

88. Ware, *Greenwich Village,* 142ff.

89. Claghorn, "Foreign Immigrant," 479–480. See also Mariano, *Second Generation Italians,* 74ff.

90. See also Oscar Handlin, *Race and Nationality in American Life* (Boston, 1957), 124ff.

91. Ware, *Greenwich Village,* 130ff.; Covello, *The Heart Is the Teacher,* 222ff.

92. John H. Finley, quoted in Adams, *Building the City,* 129, 130.

93. Thomas N. Brown, "Irish-American Nationalism: 1848–91" (Harvard University Ph.D. thesis, 1956); Florence E. Gibson, *Attitudes of the New York Irish toward State and National Affairs 1848–1892* (New York, 1951).

94. Oscar Handlin, *Al Smith and His America* (Boston, 1958), 83ff.; Ware, *Greenwich Village,* 279ff.

95. Ware, *Greenwich Village,* 152ff., 165, 200; Mariano, *Second Generation Italians,* 140ff.; Antonio Mangano, "Associated Life of the Italians in New York City," *Charities,* XII (1904), 476ff.; Oscar Handlin, *Adventure in Freedom* (New York, 1954), 109ff.; Grinstein, *Rise of the Jewish Community,* 103ff.

96. Ware, *Greenwich Village,* 304ff., 311ff.

97. Fritz A. H. Leuchs, *Early German Theatre in New York* (New York, 1928), 68ff.; Hutchins Hapgood, *Spirit of the Ghetto* (New York, 1902), 113ff.; *Charities,* XII (1904), 198, 325ff.

98. Mordecai Soltes, "The Yiddish Press," *American Jewish Year Book,* XXVI (1924–25), 174ff.; Robert E. Park, *The Immigrant Press and Its Control* (New York, 1922).

99. Ware, *Greenwich Village,* 355ff.

100. For examples, see Handlin, *Al Smith,* 11, 20ff.; Louis Marshall, *Selected Papers and Addresses* (Philadelphia, 1957), I, xivff.; Morris Hillquit, *Loose Leaves from a Busy Life* (New York, 1934); Hillel Rogoff, *An East Side Epic; the Life and Work of Meyer London* (New York, 1930); Ware, *Greenwich Village,* 270ff.

101. Handlin, *Al Smith,* 110.

102. Oscar Handlin, *American People in the Twentieth Century* (Cambridge, 1954), 121ff.; John Higham, *Strangers in the Land* (New Brunswick, 1955), 194ff.; Barbara M. Solomon, *Ancestors and Immigrants* (Cambridge, 1956), 195ff.

CHAPTER 3: THE NEWEST IMMIGRANTS

1. United States Bureau of the Census, *Special Census of April 1, 1957* (Series P–28, No. 1036). See also the reports and discussions, *New York Times,* April 7, 1957, section IV, p. 7; July 13, 1957, p. 1; October 9, 1957, pp. 1, 27; November 19, 1957, pp. 1, 27.

2. E. B. Schwulst, reported in *New York Times,* October 8, 1957.

3. N. B. Ryder, "The Reproductive Renaissance," *Annals,* CCCXVI (March, 1958), 18ff.

4. Table 10.

5. Table 11 gives aliens reporting addresses but includes many nonimmigrants.

6. William S. Bernard, *American Immigration Policy* (New York, 1950), 23ff.; Maurice R. Davie, *Refugees in America* (New York, 1947); Donald P. Kent, *Refugee Intellectual* (New York, 1953).

7. Helen F. Eckerson, "United States and Canada Magnets for Immigration," *Annals,* CCCXVI (March, 1958), 34ff.

8. Handlin, *Race and Nationality,* 223ff.; Martin A. Bursten, *Escape from Fear* (Syracuse, 1958), 50ff.

9. In general, see William Peterson, "Internal Migration and Economic Development," *Annals,* CCCXVI (March, 1958), 52ff.

10. Data from *Negro Population,* 150, 151, 156, 180, 287. The figures for the state are given in Table 12.

11. Charles H. Wesley, *Negro Labor in the United States* (New York, 1927), 55, 175, 181, 199, 208.

12. "The Negroes," U.S. Industrial Commission, *Reports on Immigration* (Washington, 1901), XV, lix; Richard O'Connor, *Hell's Kitchen* (Philadelphia, 1958), 147ff.; James W. Johnson, *Black Manhattan* (New York, 1930), 126ff.; Gunnar Myrdal, *An American Dilemma* (New York, 1944), 617ff.

13. See Table 13; Wesley, *Negro Labor,* 282ff.; Myrdal, *American Dilemma,* 182ff.

14. See Table 14; George E. Haynes, *Negro at Work in New York City* (New York, 1912), 46ff.

15. See Table 15; Haynes, *Negro at Work,* 27ff.

16. See Table 16; Haynes, *Negro at Work,* 58ff.

17. Figures from the Fifteenth, Sixteenth Censuses. See also *New York Herald Tribune,* December 1, 1957, p. 41; Chester Rapkin, *Group Relations in Newark* (Newark, 1957), 10; Paul F. Cole, "Non-white Population Increases in Metropolitan Areas," American Statistical Association, *Journal,* L (1955), 296; *Fortune,* December, 1957, 144ff.; Table 14.

18. U.S. *Seventeenth Census.* See also note 1, above.

19. In general, on the Puerto Rican background, see Felix Mejias, *Condiciones de vida de las clasas jornaleras de Puerto Rico* (San Juan, 1946), 17ff., 38ff.; R. A. Manners and J. H. Steward, "The Cultural Study of Contemporary Societies: Puerto Rico," Eugenio Fernández Méndez, ed., *Portrait of a Society* (San Juan, 1956), 18ff.; C. Wright Mills, Clarence Senior, and Rose K. Goldsen, *The Puerto Rican Journey* (New York, 1950), 3ff., 49; Julian H. Steward, "Culture Patterns of Puerto Rico," *Annals,* CCLXXXV (1953), 95ff.; V. S. Clark, *et al., Porto Rico and its Problems* (Washington, 1930), 12ff.

20. Tables 17, 18; A. J. Jaffe and Elydia Fort de Ortiz, "The Human Resource—Puerto Rico's Working Force," Fernández Méndez, *Portrait of a Society,* 88ff.; S. L. Descartes, *Basic Statistics on Puerto Rico* (Washington, 1946), 3, 8–11; Lawrence R. Chenault, *Puerto Rican Migrant in New York City* (New York, 1938), 12, 13, 29. Julian H. Steward, *et al., People of Puerto Rico* (Urbana, 1956), 34ff., 64ff., 469.

21. Paul K. Hatt, *Backgrounds of Human Fertility in Puerto Rico* (Princeton, 1952), 45; Mejias, *Condiciones de vida,* 49ff., 61ff.; Chenault, *Puerto Rican Migrant,* 18; Mills, *Puerto Rican Journey,* 33.

22. Table 19; Clark, *Porto Rico,* 515ff.; Chenault, *Puerto Rican Migrant,* 53, 141.

23. Chenault, *Puerto Rican Migrant,* 45.

24. Walton Hamilton, "The Puerto Rican Economy Linked with the Mainland," *Annals,* CCLXXXV (1953), 76ff.; Ellen Padilla, *Up from Puerto Rico* (New York, 1958), 21ff.; Mills, *Puerto Rican Journey,* 22ff., 43ff.; Dan Wakefield, *Island in the City* (Boston, 1959), 23ff.

25. Tables 19, 20; *A Summary in Facts and Figures,* April, 1957, pp. 14ff.; Sidney W. Mintz, "Puerto Rican Emigration," Fernández Méndez, *Portrait of a Society,* 199ff.; Descartes, *Basic Statistics,* 7.

26. Table 21; below, note 36.

27. Jesus de Galindez, *Puerto Rico en Nueva York* (New York, c. 1951), 13ff.; Chenault, *Puerto Rican Migrant,* 56.

28. *A Summary in Facts and Figures,* April, 1957, 18; Arthur C. Gernes, *Implications of Puerto Rican Migration to the Continent Outside New York City* (San Juan, 1955), 2; Mills, *Puerto Rican Journey,* 143.

29. Tables 21, 22.

30. Hatt, *Human Fertility in Puerto Rico,* 53, 56, 79ff., 187ff., 290ff., 331ff., 378ff., 455ff., J. M. Stycos, "Family and Fertility in Puerto Rico," *American Sociological Review,* XVII (1952), 572ff.; Jaffe and Fort de Ortiz, "The Human Resource," 90; Descartes, *Basic Statistics,* 4, 5; Joseph Monserrat, *Cultural Values and the Puerto Rican* (New York, 1957), 4; Herbert Sternau, *Puerto Rico and the Puerto Ricans* (New York, 1957), 6.

31. *La Prensa,* February 14, 1958. See also Descartes, *Basic Statistics,* 25ff., 38ff.

32. See data in *A Summary in Facts and Figures,* April, 1957, pp. 12, 13; Sternau, *Puerto Rico,* 9; Descartes, *Basic Statistics,* 13, 18, 19; Mintz, "Puerto Rican Emigration," Fernández Méndez, *Portrait of a Society,* 199ff.

33. See Table 23; Myrdal, *American Dilemma,* 161ff.

34. See Myrdal, *American Dilemma,* 284ff.; Cole, "Non-White Population Increases," 295.

35. "People, Jobs and Land 1955–1975," Regional Plan Association, *Bulletin,* Number 87 (June, 1957), 20–21.

36. See chart; Mills, *Puerto Rican Journey,* 44.

37. Clarence Senior, *Dispersion of Puerto Rican Migration* (New York, 1953); Gernes, *Implications of Puerto Rican Migration,* 5, 9ff.; Sternau, *Puerto Rico,* 21.

;8. A. J. Jaffe, ed., *Puerto Rican Population of New York City* (New York, 1954), 10ff., 13, 31ff.; Beatrice Bishop Berle, *Eighty Puerto Rican Families in New York City* (New York, 1958), 139ff.; Howard G. Brunsman, *The Estimation of Population Changes for New York City* (New York, 1955), 39; Welfare and Health Council of New York City, *N.Y.C. 1955–1965—A Report to the Community* (New York, 1955), 1.

39. Morton Zeman, "A Comparative Analysis of White-Nonwhite Income Differentials in the United States" (University of Chicago Ph.D. thesis, 1955), 4, 64ff., 74ff.

40. Myrdal, *American Dilemma*, 284ff. For the Negro attitude, see also below, p. 116.

41. See Eric Williams, "Race Relations in Puerto Rico and the Virgin Islands," *Foreign Affairs*, XXII (1945), 308ff.; Charles C. Rogler, "Role of Semantics in the Study of Race Distance in Puerto Rico," *Social Forces*, XXII (1943), 448ff.; and "Morality of Race Mixing in Puerto Rico," *ibid.*, XXV (1946), 77ff.; Steward, *People of Puerto Rico*, 409ff.

CHAPTER 4: PATTERNS OF ADJUSTMENT

1. *New York Times*, October 14, 1947.

2. See, in general, for example, Amos H. Hawley, *Changing Shape of Metropolitan America* (Glencoe, 1956), 12ff.; Morton Grodzins, "The New Shame of the Cities," *Confluence*, VII (1958), 29ff.

3. See, for example, Rhetta M. Arter, *Exploring Montclair* (New York, 1956), 9, 10.

4. A. J. Jaffe and R. O. Carleton, *Occupational Mobility in the United States 1930–1960* (New York, 1954), 11.

5. E. M. Hoover and Raymond Vernon, *Anatomy of a Metropolis* (Cambridge, 1959), 183ff.; Rhetta M. Arter, *Between Two Bridges: A Study of Human Relations in the Lower East Side* (New York, 1956), 9, 11, 18; [Dan W. Dodson], *Public Education in Greenwich Village* (New York, 1954), 7, 8; Charles Abrams, *Forbidden Neighbors* (New York, 1955), 140ff.

6. See Alan Wood, "I Sell My House," *Commentary*, XXVI (1958), 383ff.; Harry Gersh, "Gentlemen's Agreement in Bronxville," *ibid.*, XXVII (1959), 109ff.; Arter, *Exploring Montclair*, 6, 9; Abrams, *Forbidden Neighbors*, 218. See also below, note 63.

7. See George E. Haynes, *Negro at Work in New York City* (New York, 1912), 69ff.; Lawrence R. Chenault, *Puerto Rican Migrant in New York City* (New York, 1938), 44, 74; *Negro Population*, 519, 522; *A Summary in Facts and Figures*, April, 1957, p. 19; Paul K. Hatt, *Background of Human Fertility in Puerto Rico* (Princeton, 1952), 85; C. Wright Mills, Clarence Senior, and Rose K. Goldsen, *The Puerto Rican Journey* (New York, 1950), 69.

8. Gunnar Myrdal, *An American Dilemma* (New York, 1944), 380. For the Negroes, see *ibid.*, 365; Charles L. Franklin, *Negro Labor Unionist of New*

York (New York, 1936), 81ff., 271ff.; Morton Zeman, "A Comparative Analysis of White-Nonwhite Income Differences in the United States" (University of Chicago Ph.D. thesis, 1955), 4ff. For the Puerto Ricans, see Chenault, *Puerto Rican Migrant*, 73, 74.

9. Zeman, "Comparative Analysis," 23, 194ff. For the Negroes, see *Ebony, The Negro Market* (Chicago, 1955), 9; New York City Commission on Intergroup Relations, *Fact Sheet on the Sharkey-Brown-Isaacs Bill* (June 7, 1957) and *Non-White Family Income in New York City 1953–54.* For the Puerto Ricans, see A. J. Jaffe, *Puerto Rican Population of New York City* (New York, 1954), 20, 23ff.; Mills, *Puerto Rican Journey*, 23, 37, 60ff., 75; Dan Wakefield, *Island in the City* (Boston, 1959), 196ff. For the fair employment practices act, see New York State Commission Against Discrimination, *Reports of Progress* (annual); "The Operation of State Fair Employment Practices Commissions," *Harvard Law Review*, LXVIII (1955), 685ff.

10. James W. Johnson, *Black Manhattan* (New York, 1930), 283; Stan Opotowsky, "Harlem," a series in *New York Post*, March 1958; Jesus de Galindez, *Puerto Rico en Nueva York* (New York, c. 1951), 25; John H. Burma, *Spanish-Speaking Groups in the United States* (Durham, 1954), 164ff.

11. J. L. Roman, "Raquets de Nueva York," *El Diario de Nueva York*, March 26, 1957 ff.; *New York Amsterdam News*, August 23, 1958, p. 1; below, p. 102; above, p. 37. Myrdal is in error in the statement that Negroes started policy in New York (*American Dilemma*, 330, 331). Its history in the city reaches back to the first half of the nineteenth century.

12. This statement is based upon an examination of the publications listed below, p. 106, through 1957 and 1958. See also Johnson, *Black Manhattan*, 74ff., 175ff.

13. See *La Prensa*, February 4, 1958, pp. 2, 3; also George E. Haynes, *Negro at Work in New York City* (New York, 1912), 101ff.

14. *New York Amsterdam News*, March 15, 1958; Jaffe, *Puerto Rican Population*, 57, 59–61.

15. Myrdal, *American Dilemma*, 307ff.; Haynes, *Negro at Work in New York City*, 99; Christopher Rand, *The Puerto Ricans* (New York, 1958), 37ff.

16. These examples are from *Jet*, April 11, 1957, p. 6, July 4, 1957, p. 47, January 29, 1958, pp. 42, 50ff., August 7, 1958, p. 44; *Ebony*, August, 1957, p. 35. See also Myrdal, *American Dilemma*, 367ff.

17. See MacCoby and Fulder, "Savings among Upper-Income Families in Puerto Rico," Fernández Méndez, *Portrait of a Society*, 81ff.; Elena Padilla, *Up from Puerto Rico* (New York, 1958), 153ff.; Julian H. Steward, *et al., People of Puerto Rico* (Urbana, 1956), 241.

18. Edmund D. Cronon, *Black Moses, The Story of Marcus Garvey* (Madison, 1955), 50ff.

19. See, for example, Gary S. Becker, *Economics of Discrimination* (Chicago, 1957), 77.

20. For attitudes in Puerto Rico, see Paul K. Hatt, *Backgrounds of Human Fertility in Puerto Rico* (Princeton, 1952), 76–78; for New York, see special

supplement, *La Prensa,* January 29, 1958; *Westchester County Press,* June 29, 1957.

21. See above, note 9; below, Chapter 5, note 3.

22. New York State Commission Against Discrimination, *Employment in the Hotel Industry* (report of March 1958); and *Puerto Rican Employment in New York City Hotels* (report of October 1958); *New York Amsterdam News,* April 19, 1958; SCAD *Newsletter,* II, No. 2 (March 1959), 2.

23. See, in general, Zeman, "Comparative Analysis," 108, 112ff.

24. See Padilla, *Up from Puerto Rico,* 198ff.; Mills, *Puerto Rican Journey,* 161ff.; Steward, *People of Puerto Rico,* 481ff.

25. See, for example, *Jet,* April 11, 1957, p. 24, August 7, 1958, p. 42; *Ebony,* April, 1957, pp. 83ff.; Wakefield, *Island in the City,* 149ff.

26. See statistics in *Negro Population,* 388.

27. See statistics in *Negro Population,* 415; also J. Cayce Morrison, *The Puerto Rican Study 1953–1957* (New York, 1958), 110; *A Summary in Facts and Figures,* April 1957, p. 6; Joseph Monserrat, *Background and General Information on Puerto Rico* (New York, 1952), 2; Trumbull White, *Puerto Rico and Its People* (New York, 1937), 209ff.; V. S. Clark, *et al., Porto Rico and Its Problems* (Washington, 1930), 73ff.; Jaffe, *Puerto Rican Population,* 17; Dan W. Dodson, *Between Hell's Kitchen and San Juan Hill* (New York, 1952), 25.

28. Padilla, *Up from Puerto Rico,* 210; Morrison, *Puerto Rican Study,* 117, 129, 142.

29. Reported in *New York Times,* January 6, 1958. See also Tables 24–26; Morrison, *Puerto Rican Study,* 152ff., 172ff.; Jaffe, *Puerto Rican Population,* 50, 51.

30. On the problems of the Puerto Ricans, see Morrison, *Puerto Rican Study,* 13ff.; Clarence Senior, *Strangers and Neighbors* (New York, 1952), 38, 39; Padilla, *Up from Puerto Rico,* 201ff. On the Negro reaction, see, for example, *New York Amsterdam News,* March 15, 1958, p. 1, for the problems in P.S. 2 and P.S. 70 in the Bronx. See also, William Jansen, Superintendent of Schools, *Report #1 on Integration* (New York, 1957); *New York Times,* September 30, 1957, pp. 1, 25, October 6, 1957, sec. IV, p. 5.

31. See M. M. Tumin and A. S. Feldman, "Status, Perspective and Achievement: Education and Class Structure in Puerto Rico," *American Sociological Review,* XXI (1956), 464ff.; Morrison, *Puerto Rican Study,* 129, 142.

32. Table 27; Haynes, *Negro at Work in New York,* 48ff.

33. See Myrdal, *American Dilemma,* 1125ff.; Haynes, *Negro at Work in New York,* 62ff.; *Negro Population,* 463; T. J. Woofter, Jr., *Negro Problems in Cities* (New York, 1928), 48; Johnson, *Black Manhattan,* 146ff.; Leo Grebler, *Housing Market Behavior in a Declining Area. Long-Term Changes in Inventory and Utilization of Housing on New York's Lower East Side* (New York, 1952), 15ff., 148ff.

34. Frederick Woltman, "The Fabulous No. 409," *Negro Digest,* IX (June 1951), 87ff.; Woofter, *Negro Problems in Cities,* 115ff.

35. Owen R. Lovejoy, *Negro Children of New York* (New York, 1932), 18ff., 20; Woofter, *Negro Problems in Cities*, 49, 87, 128ff.

36. On public housing, see Abrams, *Forbidden Neighbors*, 150ff., 229ff.; Myrdal, *American Dilemma*, 348; on the disregard of ethnic considerations in planning, see, for example, Clarence A. Perry, *The Rebuilding of Blighted Areas* (New York, 1933).

37. *New York Times*, June 23, August 2, 1943.

38. Welfare and Health Council of New York City, *The Present Housing Emergency in N.Y.C.* (April, 1953), 1; Abrams, *Forbidden Neighbors*, 70ff.; Hoover and Vernon, *Anatomy of a Metropolis*, 196ff.

39. Based on 1950 housing census. In writing this section, I have profited by the ability to read the draft of *Housing and Minorities*, the final report to the Commission on Race and Housing by Davis McEntire and staff. The opinions expressed are my own, however.

40. From data in the 1950 housing census. See also *New York Times*, October 20, 1958. See also Gary S. Becker, *Economics of Discrimination* (Chicago, 1957), 61, 62.

41. Table 28; Chester Rapkin, *Group Relations in Newark* (Newark, 1957), 10; report of a survey by the Mayor's Commission on Group Relations, *New York Times*, September 30, 1957, April 3, 1959, p. 29; *Human Relations News* (Newark), May 1959.

42. Table 29; see also New York City Housing Authority, *Twenty-Second Annual Report* (New York, 1955).

43. See the report of Charles F. Preusse, city administrator, reported in *New York Times*, September 23, 1957.

44. Based on maps available at the Office of Master Planning, Department of City Planning, City of New York in the Street or Tenant Relocation Study of 1953.

45. Adopted January 20, 1954. See Sec. 105c, Title I, 1949 Housing Act.

46. New York City Planning Commission, *Tenant Relocation Report* (New York, 1954), 9.

47. *Ibid.*, 4, 5.

48. *Ibid.*, 6.

49. *Ibid.*, 11, 13.

50. Press release of boards nos. 9, 10, 11 at the Harlem Y.M.C.A. (September 1957).

51. New York City Commission on Intergroup Relations, *Non-White Family Income*.

52. Data from Temporary State Housing Rent Commission, *Incomes and Ability to Pay for Housing of Non-White Families in New York State*, (1954), 14.

53. See Dorsey v. Stuyvesant Town Corp. (1949), 299 N.Y.S. 12, 87 N.E. 571; Abrams, *Forbidden Neighbors*, 251ff.; the text of the Brown-Sharkey-Isaacs Law is in New York City Administrative Code, Sec. 1, Chapter 41, Title X; and *New York Times*, December 6, 1957. See also "Discrimination in

Housing—a Debate," *New York Times Magazine,* July 21, 1957, p. 52; *New York Times,* December 8, 1957, sec. 8, p. 1; State Commission Against Discrimination, Division of Housing, *Legislation on Discrimination in Housing* (New York, 1956).

54. See the advertisement for canvassers, *Tan,* November, 1958, p. 3.

55. See Morgan Belden, "Values in Transition Areas," *Review of Society of Residential Appraisers* (Chicago), March, 1952, 5-10; Hoover and Vernon, *Anatomy of a Metropolis,* 210.

56. Interviews with Joseph Davis, executive vice-president, Carver Savings and Loan Association and President Richard Brennan of the Brevoort Savings Bank. See also statement of E. B. Schwulst of the Bowery Savings Bank, *New York Times,* October 8, 1957.

57. See Appendix; also Abrams, *Forbidden Neighbors,* 273.

58. Abrams, *Forbidden Neighbors,* 274ff., 315ff.

59. See, for example, Urban League, *Memorandum on Housing Policy* (September, 1955), 7; *Jet,* July 24, 1958, p. 9; *New York Times,* October 12, 13, November 21, 22, 1959; Frank Horne, "The Open City—Threshold to American Maturity," *Phylon Quarterly,* XX (1957), 135.

60. Buell Gallagher, Sermon at Cathedral of St. John the Divine, *New York Times,* October 7, 1957; Abrams, *Forbidden Neighbors,* 279ff.

61. The study of shifts in residents (see Appendix) reveals that only two of the eighty-two persons involved moved to be nearer their place of employment.

62. See, for example, Rhetta M. Arter, *Exploring Montclair* (New York, 1956), 7, 8, 13; also *supra,* notes 34, 41. On the Negroes in Westchester, see, The Housing Council, *Westchester's Non-white Population, 1957—a Preliminary Analysis* (White Plains, 1957); Urban League of Westchester County, *The Non-White Population of Mt. Vernon, N.Y.* (White Plains, 1958); Westchester County Council of Social Agencies, *Report of the Committee on Housing* (White Plains, July 1957). While this manuscript was in press, the New York State Commission against Discrimination issued its Trend Report No. 3 (June 1959), *Nonwhites in New York's Four "Suburban" Counties,* a helpful analysis which, in general, confirms the position taken above.

63. See Cooperative Committee on Open Occupancy Listings, *Listings for New York City, Suffolk, Westchester and Rockland Counties,* No. 2 (April, 1957); and, in general, Abrams, *Forbidden Neighbors,* 169ff.

64. "Residential Proximity and Intergroup Relations in Public Housing," *Journal of Social Issues,* VIII (1952), 45; "Where Can a Negro Live," *Hartford Courant,* August 19-25, 1957.

65. See Appendix.

66. See Arter, *Exploring Montclair,* 14.

67. See August Meier, "Race Relations at Negro Colleges," *Crisis,* LXV (November 1958), 535ff.

68. "People, Jobs and Land 1955–1975," *Regional Plan Association Bulletin,* No. 87 (June 1957), 1-14, 70.

69. Chenault, *Puerto Rican Migrant*, 90ff.; Trumbull White, *Puerto Rico and Its People* (New York, 1937), 26off.

70. Mejias, *Condiciones de vida*, 136ff.; Chenault, *Puerto Rican Migrant*, 98ff.

71. Based on data in Puerto Rican Health Area Schedule, New York City Department of City Planning, Office of Master Planning. See also Table 31; Dodson, *Between Two Bridges*, 9, 12.

72. Jaffe, *Puerto Rican Population*, 49ff.; Martin B. Dworkis, *Impact of Puerto Rican Migration on Government Services in New York City* (New York, 1957), 9ff.; Beatrice Bishop Berle, *Eighty Puerto Rican Families in New York City* (New York, 1958), 46, 47, 92ff.; Dodson, *Between Hell's Kitchen and San Juan Hill*, 16, 17; Padilla, *Up from Puerto Rico*, 7; Abrams, *Forbidden Neighbors*, 60–63; Mills, *Puerto Rican Journey*, 92ff.; Wakefield, *Island in the City*, 235.

73. Padilla, *Up from Puerto Rico*, 6; Burma, *Spanish-Speaking Groups*, 162ff.; *New York Times*, April 3, 1959, p. 29.

74. See Erwin Schepses, "Puerto Rican Delinquent Boys in New York City," *Social Service Review*, XXIII (1949), 59.

75. See, in general, Arnold Rose, "The Problem of the Mass Society," *Theory and Methods in the Social Sciences* (Minneapolis, 1954), 25ff.; Marshall B. Clinard, *Sociology of Deviant Behavior* (New York, 1957), 54ff.

76. New York City Youth Board, *An Experiment in the Validation of the Glueck Predication Scale. Progress Report from November 1952 to December 1956* (New York, 1957).

77. Mejias, *Condiciones de vida*, 45, 156ff.; *A Summary in Facts and Figures*, April 1957, p. 4; V. S. Clark, *Porto Rico and Its Problems* (Washington, 1930), 55ff.; Chenault, *Puerto Rican Migrant*, 40, 110ff., 115; Dworkis, *Impact of Puerto Rican Migration*, 45ff.

78. See Russell Sage Foundation, Committee on Statistical Program for the City of New York, *Statistical Program for the Department of Health* (New York, 1956), 39; Woofter, *Negro Problems in Cities*, 92; *Negro Population* (1910), 350, 351; Lovejoy, *Negro Children*, 27ff.; Chenault, *Puerto Rican Migrant*, 116; Berle, *Eighty Puerto Rican Families*, 148, 172ff.

79. See, in general, Mortimer Spiegelman, "Mortality Trends and Prospects," *Annals of the American Academy of Political and Social Science*, CCXVI (1958), 25ff.; *Negro Population*, 298ff., 319, 320; Jaffe, *Puerto Rican Population*, 12ff., 35ff.; Dodson, *Between Hell's Kitchen and San Juan Hill*, 18, 19.

80. There is an excellent analysis of New York State data, with a lucid summary by Dorothy S. Thomas, of earlier literature in Benjamin Malzberg and Everett S. Lee, *Migration and Mental Disease* (New York, 1956), especially, 31, 74ff.

81. Berle, *Eighty Puerto Rican Families*, 156ff., 205ff.; Padilla, *Up from Puerto Rico*, 279ff.

82. Sophia M. Robison, *Can Delinquency Be Measured?* (New York, 1937),

21ff.; Milton L. Barron, *The Juvenile in Delinquent Society* (New York, 1954), 32, 41, 56, 67; Alfred J. Kahn, *A Court for Children* (New York, 1953); *Young People in the Courts of New York State* (Legislative Document No. 55 of 1942).

83. There is a recent journalistic survey in Harrison E. Salisbury, "Youth," *New York Times*, March 24, 1958ff. See also Padilla, *Up from Puerto Rico*, 226ff.; Wakefield, *Island in the City*, 117ff.

84. Schepses, "Puerto Rican Delinquent Boys," 51ff.; Jaffe, *Puerto Rican Population*, 52ff.

85. Barron, *The Juvenile*, 63ff., 161; Norman Podhoretz, "The Know-Nothing Bohemians," *Partisan Review*, XXV (1958), 476; Wakefield, *Island in the City*, 122.

86. See maps, *Perspectives on Delinquency Prevention* (New York, 1955), 22, 23, 28; New York City Youth Board, *Experiment;* Barron, *The Juvenile*, 161, 228ff.; Lovejoy, *Negro Children*, 37; Jaffe, *Puerto Rican Population*, 52; Chenault, *Puerto Rican Migrants*, 136, 137; Richard E. Harris, *Delinquency in Our Democracy* (Los Angeles, 1954), 35ff.; Dworkis, *Impact of Puerto Rican Migration*, 54ff.

87. These theories are adequately summarized in Barron, *The Juvenile*, 106ff., 128ff., 150ff., 186ff.; see also Sheldon and Eleanor Glueck, *Unravelling Juvenile Delinquency* (New York, 1950), 4ff., 107, 167; *Perspectives on Delinquency Prevention*, 8.

88. See, for example, "Teen-Age Cheat," *Tan*, January, 1959; "I Led a Girl's Gang," *ibid.*, November, 1957, 15ff.; "Too Young to Marry," *ibid.*, November 1957, 8ff.

89. See Myrdal, *American Dilemma*, 974ff.; Padilla, *Up from Puerto Rico*, 44ff.; Chenault, *Puerto Rican Migrant*, 140; *Negro Population*, 437; *New York Amsterdam News*, August 23, 1958, p. 1; Wakefield, *Island in the City*, 119.

90. Jaffe, *Puerto Rican Population*, 46ff.; Chenault, *Puerto Rican Migrant*, 85; Senior, *Strangers and Neighbors*, 38, 39; Berle, *Eighty Puerto Rican Families*, 116ff.; Burma, *Spanish-Speaking Groups*, 163; Galindez, *Puerto Rico*, 17; Padilla, *Up from Puerto Rico*, 258ff.; Mills, *Puerto Rican Journey*, 80ff.

91. See "How to Win at the Races," *Ebony*, August 1957, 41ff.; *El Diario de Nueva York*, March 24, 1957, p. 2; *Jet*, July 3, 1958, 45; Galindez, *Puerto Rico*, 42; Earl Brown, "The Numbers Business," *New York Amsterdam News*, May 24, 1958, p. 10; above, p. 71.

92. See, for example, *Jet*, April 11, 1957, p. 21, January 9, 1958, pp. 18–21, 43, July 24, 1958, pp. 44, 48; *El Diario de Nueva York*, March 24, 1957, pp. 2, 3; Galindez, *Puerto Rico*, 48ff.; Dr. Thomasa-Sanchez, *La Prensa*, May 21, 1957, p. 4; Padilla, *Up from Puerto Rico*, 242ff.; Wakefield, *Island in the City*, 41, 87ff.

93. On the Puerto Rican family, see Reuben Hill, "Impediments to Freedom of Mate Selection in Puerto Rico," Fernández Méndez, *Portrait of a*

Society, 55ff.; Kathleen L. Wolf, "Growing Up and Its Price in Three Puerto Rican Sub-Cultures," *Psychiatry,* XV (1952), 401ff.; Padilla, *Up from Puerto Rico,* 62ff., 101ff., 150ff., 169ff.; Berle, *Eighty Puerto Rican Families,* 72ff.; Hatt, *Backgrounds of Human Fertility in Puerto Rico,* 61ff.; Burma, *Spanish-Speaking Groups,* 171, 172, 176ff. Popular fiction is informative on the strains in the Negro family. See, for example, "We Had to Have Each Other," *Tan,* January, 1959, pp. 17ff.; "Anything to Keep His Love," *ibid.,* 30ff.; "A Mother But Not A Wife," *ibid.,* 39ff.; "The Curse I Lived With," *ibid.,* November 1957, pp. 27ff. See also, in general, E. Franklin Frazier, *Negro Family in the United States* (Chicago, 1939). On the relationship to particular disorders, see Malzberg and Lee, *Migration and Mental Disease,* 92.

94. See, for example, Marvin K. Opler, "Dilemmas of Two Puerto Rican Men," G. Seward, ed., *Clinical Studies in Culture Conflict* (New York, 1958), 223ff.; Berle, *Eighty Puerto Rico Families,* 64ff.; "This Hate Inside," *Tan,* November 1957, pp. 25ff.

CHAPTER 5: FORMS OF SOCIAL ACTION

1. Elena Padilla, *Up from Puerto Rico* (New York, 1958), 212ff.; C. Wright Mills, Clarence Senior, and Rose K. Goldsen, *The Puerto Rican Journey* (New York, 1950), 105ff.

2. See Jesus de Galindez, *Puerto Rico en Nueva York* (New York, c. 1951), 55ff.; *La Prensa,* June 21, 1958, p. 2.

3. Events are chronicled in the columns, Sonia Ellis, "Sociales," and Gonzalo Jusino, "Nueva York Hispano" in *El Diario de Nueva York.* See also Galindez, *Puerto Rico,* 53ff.; Mitchel Levitas, "New York's Labor Scandal: the Puerto Rican Workers," *New York Post,* July 15, 1957, p. M8. Felix Mejias, *Condiciones de vida de las clasas jornaleras de Puerto Rico* (San Juan, 1946), 68ff.; *La Prensa,* May 22, 1958; Council of Spanish-American Organizations of Greater New York, *A Self-Help Manual on Housing Problems* (New York, [1957]); James W. Johnson, *Black Manhattan* (New York, 1930), 167ff.; Gunnar Myrdal, *An American Dilemma* (New York, 1944), 952; Mills, *The Puerto Rican Journey,* 109ff.; Dan Wakefield, *Island in the City* (Boston, 1959), 205; Julian H. Steward, *et al., People of Puerto Rico* (Urbana, 1956), 77ff., 479ff.; Charles L. Franklin, *Negro Labor Unionist of New York* (New York, 1936), 159ff.

4. See *Jet,* July 3, 1958, p. 20, August 7, 1958, p. 63, August 14, 1958; "America's Black Jews," *Ebony,* May 1957, pp. 96ff.; *New York Amsterdam News,* May 24, 1958, pp. 1, 21, 24; Johnson, *Black Manhattan,* 163ff.; Langston Hughes, *Tambourines to Glory* (New York, John Day, 1958); Myrdal, *An American Dilemma,* 935ff. See also the advertisement for psalm prayer candles, *Tan,* January, 1959, p. 9.

5. See Paul K. Hatt, *Backgrounds of Human Fertility in Puerto Rico* (Princeton, 1952), 39ff.; Steward, *People of Puerto Rico,* 84ff., 475ff.

6. See Galindez, *Puerto Rico,* 29ff., 56ff.; Beatrice Bishop Berle, *Eighty*

Puerto Rican Families in New York City (New York, 1958), 53ff.; Padilla, *Up from Puerto Rico,* 124ff., 273, 283, 291ff. See also M. M. Tumin and A. S. Feldman, "Miracle at Sabana Grande," *Public Opinion Quarterly,* XIX (1955); Mills, *The Puerto Rican Journey,* 110ff.; Wakefield, *Island in the City,* 49ff.; Steward, *People of Puerto Rico,* 127.

7. See, for example, *La Prensa,* May 21, 1957; also Galindez, *Puerto Rico,* 40ff.; Mills, *The Puerto Rican Journey,* 117ff., 119; John H. Burma, *Spanish-Speaking Groups in the United States* (Durham, 1954), 167. The mass media, of course, have also had a wide influence in Latin America itself. See, for example, *La Esfera* (Caracas), May 7, 1957.

8. See *La Prensa,* July 21, 1957; Hospital Council of Greater New York, *Bulletin,* XII (September 1957), No. 4, p. 3; Padilla, *Up from Puerto Rico,* 191; Berle, *Eighty Puerto Rican Families,* 80; Dora Tannenbaum, Sara McCaulley, and H. D. Carpenter, *The Puerto Rican Migration* (New York, 1955), 10.

9. See James L. Hicks, "Leadership," *New York Amsterdam News,* May 24, 1958, p. 1; Myrdal, *An American Dilemma,* 1133ff.; Berle, *Eighty Puerto Rican Families,* 105ff.; Tannenbaum, McCaulley, and Carpenter, *Puerto Rican Migration,* 6; Padilla, *Up from Puerto Rico,* 250ff.; Mills, *The Puerto Rican Journey,* 107.

10. "Nation's Most Beautiful Debs," *Ebony,* April, 1957, pp. 27, 28; *New York Amsterdam News,* August 23, 1958, p. 6. See also Adelaide Hill, "The Negro Upper Class in Boston" (Radcliffe College Ph.D. thesis, 1952).

11. See *Jet,* July 24, 1958, p. 45.

12. Stan Opotowsky, "Harlem," a series in *New York Post,* March 1958.

13. See Edmund D. Cronon, *Black Moses the Story of Marcus Garvey* (Madison, 1955), 50ff.; *New York Amsterdam News,* August 23, 1958, p. 7; James W. Johnson, *Black Manhattan* (New York, 1930), 156, 157, 231ff.

14. Charles S. Braden, *These Also Believe* (New York, 1951), 1ff.

15. See, *New-York Amsterdam News,* May 24, 1958, pp. 1, 10, August 23, 1958, p. 8; also *Jet,* June 12, 1958, 10–13 and cover.

16. See *La Prensa,* July 3, 1957, 3, May 22, 1958, 3; Padilla, *Up from Puerto Rico,* 35ff.

17. See *La Prensa,* May 21, 1957, p. 2, July 3, 1957, p. 3, June 21, 1958, p. 2; Padilla, *Up from Puerto Rico,* 32ff., 48, 73ff., 95; Rhetta M. Arter, *Between Two Bridges* (New York, 1956), 19, 36; Mills, *The Puerto Rican Journey,* 132ff.; Wakefield, *Island in the City,* 40ff.

18. Padilla, *Up from Puerto Rico,* 89ff.

19. Myrdal, *American Dilemma,* 927ff.

20. These examples are from *Tan,* November 1958; *Ebony,* April 1957, p. 27; *New York Amsterdam News,* August 23, 1958, p. 3.

21. *Jet,* April 11, 1957, p. 39.

22. See, for example, "God Forbade Our Marriage," *Tan,* November 1957, pp. 36ff.; "Love Across the Color Line," *ibid.,* November 1958, pp. 22ff.

23. Elijah Muhammad, "Islamic World," *New York Amsterdam News,* March 15, 1958, p. 15.

24. Padilla, *Up from Puerto Rico,* 53ff., 93ff., 96; Mills, *The Puerto Rican Journey,* 126ff.; Wakefield, *Island in the City,* 180ff.

25. Burma, *Spanish-Speaking Groups,* 173; Galindez, *Puerto Rico,* 51ff.

26. See Padilla, *Up from Puerto Rico,* 86, 255; Mills, *The Puerto Rican Journey,* 108; also *Jet,* 1958, pp. 14, 30.

27. *New York Amsterdam News,* March 15, 1958, p. 1; also Myrdal, *American Dilemma,* 819ff., 837ff., 908ff.

28. *Jet,* April 4, 1957, pp. 38, 57.

29. *Jet,* April 4, 1957, pp. 14–15; *Ebony,* August 1957, pp. 65ff.

30. See, for example, Melvin Tapley, "Our People, Pages from History," *New York Amsterdam News,* March 15, 1958, p. 7; the regular series, "Yesterday in Negro History," *Jet;* Cronon, *Black Moses,* 209ff.; Myrdal, *American Dilemma,* 752ff.

31. See *Jet,* April 4, 1957, p. 20; July 31, 1958, August 7, 1958, p. 8.

32. *El Diario de Nueva York,* March 24, 1957, p. 8; *La Prensa,* May 2, 1957, May 22, 1958; Wakefield, *Island in the City,* 249ff.

33. See *La Prensa,* February 4, 1958, p. 8, May 22, 1958, p. 2; *New York Amsterdam News,* March 15, 1958, p. 10. For the allocation of Youth Board funds to private agencies, see also *Perspectives on Delinquency Prevention,* 50, 51.

Index